SURVIVAL, GROWTH AND PERPETUITY
Odebrecht Entrepreneurial Technology

Norberto Odebrecht

Translated by H. Sabrina Gledhill

Odebrecht Foundation
Av. Luiz Viana Filho, 2841, Ed. Odebrecht, Salvador,
Bahia, Brazil

1st Portuguese edition (1983)
1st English edition (1985)
2nd Portuguese edition (1987)
1st Spanish edition (1990)
2nd Spanish edition (1984)
2nd English edition (1993)
3rd Portuguese edition (1998)
3rd English edition (1998)
3rd Spanish edition (1998)
4th Portuguese edition (2002)
5th Portuguese edition (2004)
4th English edition (2005)

	Odebrecht, Norberto, 1920-
023	Survival, Growth and Perpetuity: Odebrecht Entrepreneurial Technology / Norberto Odebrecht: translated by H. Sabrina Gledhill. 4th edition. vol. 1. Salvador: Odebrecht, 1983. 3 vol.
	ISBN – 85-8502361-9
	1. Administration. 2. Entrepreneurial philosophy. 1. Gledhill, H. Sabrina, trans. II. Title
	CDD – 658.001
	CDU – 65.01

To those who trust me.

A note from the Author

This **edition** of *Survival, Growth and Perpetuity* was necessary, first and foremost, because the previous edition is out of print.

Although most of the people who acquire this book are Members of the organization, it has received a warm welcome from Students of Business Administration and other Companies interested in the practice of **decentralization, planned delegation** and **partnership.**

Secondly, this edition has been released to eliminate some proofreading errors and particularly to correct **Figure 6.1.**

In the previous edition, this figure did not adequately illustrate the fact that the **Client** and **Shareholder** are situated **outside** the organization, and that it is up to the Entrepreneur to harmonize and synergize the interests of these two **living forces,** to which the organization owes its existence.

In this regard, it should be stressed that Entrepreneurs are responsible for laying the groundwork for a **positive-sum game** and putting it into practice. This is a **"win-win"** situation that must simultaneously benefit the Client, Shareholders, the People who Serve them and the Community at large.

Otherwise, this Edition remains unchanged and has not adopted any of the "buzz words" that periodically arise in the active "market" of lecture circuits and books on business management. Until they are rightly forgotten, these terms will only serve to disrupt the correct understanding of what the **art of entrepreneurship** is all about.

Among these "buzz words," one that merits the greatest criticism is the term *gestão* ("management"), which, in Portuguese, means "running other people's businesses." According to the Odebrecht Entrepreneurial Technology (TEO), Entrepreneurs do not run other people's businesses. They run their **own Businesses** and **view the organization as their own.**

Another term that has been proliferating in Brazil, clearly as a result of mistranslation, is *corporação* ("corporation"). In Portuguese, it designates archaic medieval guilds, and *corporativismo* ("cronyism") is a tendency for a closed group to benefit itself alone, to the detriment of the rest of the Community.

Another term is "competitiveness" which, when used heedlessly, can confuse younger people and lead them to believe that the entrepreneurial life is a "perpetual war, with everyone against everyone"; a zero- or negative-sum game that creates "win-lose" or even "lose-lose" situations.

Naturally, Entrepreneurs must behave like **warriors** in the constant struggle to **give more and better Service.**

In the course of this constant struggle, Entrepreneurs must be aware that the greatest enemies of total productivity are not "external"; they are found inside their own organization, as has been shown in **The Success Trap.**

Before being warriors, however, Entrepreneurs must be **diplomats** in order to set in motion and successfully play a **positive-sum game** and form a win-win relationship between their organization and the Outside World, thereby helping establish and reinforce a **Partnership of Trust.**

This is increasingly true to the extent that each Entrepreneur proves to be a **provider of unique, individualized services.**

In the hope that the Reader will always remain on guard against "buzz words," it should be recalled that the following maxim by Brazilian jurist Rui Barbosa is perfectly valid in the field of **entrepreneurship:**

In the moral world, as in the physical world, change rests on a changeless foundation.

Salvador, September 2002

Norberto Odebrecht

We do not learn, Lord, through fantasy,
by dreaming, imagining or studying,
but by seeing, confronting and grappling.
Canto X, verse 153

Let cease all that the ancient Muse doth sing
That another, finer value may take wing.
Canto I, verse 3

Camoens, *The Lusiads*

SURVIVAL, GROWTH AND PERPETUITY
Odebrecht Entrepreneurial Technology

CONTENTS

PART II | STANDARDS FOR APPLYING THE ODEBRECHT
ENTREPRENEURIAL TECHNOLOGY ....

CHAPTER 3
GENERAL STANDARDS ....

CHAPTER 4

The first edition of this book dates back to 1982.

Since then, the world has changed, every one of us has changed, and so has the Odebrecht Group.

The jurist, orator and statesman Ruy Barbosa once said, **"everything changes on the basis of a changeless foundation."**

What has remained changeless for the Odebrecht Group?

Although their form has been adapted, the **Principles, Concepts and Standards** that comprise the pillars of the **Odebrecht Entrepreneurial Technology** have remained essentially changeless.

As a result, the Shareholders' **spirit of service** remains the source of inspiration for the Leaders and their Team Members, both Line Members and those whose mission is to provide Support, as will be explained further on.

As in the past, the **spirit of service** is manifested through the commitment to generating more and better wealth for Clients, the Communities, and particularly for the end Users of services and goods produced by the Odebrecht Group, as well as for its Shareholders and Members.

Other qualities that must remain changeless are the **humility** and **simplicity** of the Group's Members, as these virtues are inherent to those whose **duty** and **pleasure** is to **serve**.

As always, we must fight – and cut off at the roots – any signs of the "arrogance" and "condescension" which are so common among people who have allowed themselves to be ensnared by the "success trap."

In this case, the best antidote is **constant dissatisfaction** with the **results** achieved.

No matter how good the results may be, we must **surpass** them, **today, tomorrow** and **always**.

An **Entrepreneurial Technology** is the set of tools which Shareholders place at the Entrepreneurs' disposal so that they can **coordinate** the work of Human Beings who are experts in the specific technologies needed to satisfy the Client, **integrate** them into synergetic and contributive Teams and lead them to produce **more** and **better moral** and **material wealth** that is available to the Client and the Community.

When working with these tools, the Entrepreneur will perceive that it is necessary to adapt them to the specific requirements of his business and circumstances in order to use them as productively as possible.

This takes place with any technology that is perfected through interaction between **accumulated knowledge** and **new knowledge** produced from day to day through **practice**, and particularly through **communication** with the Client, Suppliers, Leaders and Team Members.

. . .

The **practice of entrepreneurship** is guided primarily by **intuition. To reflect** on this practice in search of its inherent **logic** requires the help of **reasoning.**

When reflecting on what he does, the Entrepreneur brings about – in his own mind – a **dynamic balance** between **intuition** and **reason,** while stimulating the simultaneous development of these two components of his intellect.

By devoting himself to reflection on **present** and **future results,** the Entrepreneur engages in **self development** while contributing to the **development** of his co-workers.

I believe that the **spoken word** is the most suitable instrument for encouraging **intuitive thinking,** while the **written word** plays a similar role in the case of **rational thinking.**

Therefore, since the 1940s I have become accustomed to using the written word to reflect on specific situations that have arisen in the course of the relationship between the Group's Members and their Clients, Users and Partners in the Communities we serve.

The documents thus generated, which are always **succinct,** written in **direct language in short, pithy sentences,** have formed the basis for the creative meetings I habitually hold with the People whom I interrelate with directly.

One after the other, these documents have developed an **active history** in which the **past** helps clarify the **present** and both, in their turn, interact to **build the future.**

These individual documents are inherently consistent, because they arise from

- a single **culture applied** on a daily basis and indistinguishable from the commitment to **give service first in order to be served later on**; and

- the same method of thinking: **intuition** sets the **strategy** and is later adapted to suit the dictates of reason.

Every time an opportunity arises to take a leap forward in the Odebrecht Group's **organic** and **healthy growth**, it seems useful to systematize these documents and publish them in book form.

That was the case when:

- in 1968 ***De que Necessitamos?*** (What do We Need?) helped explain the Odebrecht Group's Philosophical Concepts as well as the **ethics** and **morals** on which they are based. This book was extremely valuable because it helped consolidate what was then the Large Firm as a **Federation of Small Firms** on the basis of **decentralization, planned delegation** and **partnership**;

- in 1970, ***Pontos de Referência*** (Points of Reference) became a guide for the next generation of Entrepreneurs, who were committed to making Odebrecht a national organization in its country of origin;

- in 1981, ***Survival, Growth and Perpetuity***, expanded in 1984 and revised in 1986, formulated what we had decided to call the **Odebrecht Entrepreneurial Technology,** as well as helping **systemize** the habit, followed since the Group's beginnings, of working from the basis of **Action Plans** and **Programs;**

■ and in 1991, ***Education through Work*** emerged. Its title was chosen to place a high value on the Odebrecht Group's Leaders' commitment to passing on the organization's Technology to the next generations of Entrepreneurs. This book confirmed the awareness heralded in ***Pontos de Referência*** that Odebrecht must function as a **Group made up of Knowledgeable People.**

■ ■ ■

As President and CEO and later Chairman of the Board, I always kept a close eye on the achievements of the Group's Entrepreneurs.

However, it was only in August 1995, at a meeting held to mark the Odebrecht Group's first 50 years, that I became fully aware of its responsibilities in an increasingly **integrated** world.

On that occasion, I had the opportunity to listen to and be heard by **Young Entrepreneurs** who form part of the Group. They came from several different countries and shared the true **spirit of service.**

This meeting made my **sense of responsibility** even keener with the aim of helping the **spirit** of these Entrepreneurs – wherever they may be – find the right conditions for blossoming and becoming useful to the Clients, Users and Communities we serve, as well as Shareholders and Group Members.

I became aware that I had to formulate messages that **transcend boundaries** to reinforce what is essential within the Odebrecht Group:

> *the spirit of service,*

which the Leaders, through their **entrepreneurial spirit**, must pass on to their Team Members and convert into **team spirit**.

I would like to point out the difference between the **spirit of service, entrepreneurial spirit** and **team spirit**.

In addition to the **spirit of service**, every Entrepreneur has **grit, determination**, the desire to **live life intensely**, the **unwavering commitment** to **success**, and the willingness to convert **problems** into **opportunities** and, through **maturity**, acquire the capacity to bring about a **dynamic balance** between **intuition** and **reason**.

When combined with the **spirit of service**, I believe that these **virtues** constitute the **entrepreneurial spirit**.

And, to the extent that he passes on the **entrepreneurial spirit** to his Team Members, the Entrepreneur will create **team spirit**.

. . .

For over a decade, the Odebrecht Group's Shareholders have been encouraging the **diversification** of its investments, particularly into Chemicals and Petrochemicals.

Investments in Tangible Assets and particularly Intangible Assets, which are the identification, acculturation and integration of **new and better Entrepreneurs** who have a full **mastery of** the **Odebrecht Entrepreneurial Technology** and the **specific technologies for** their Businesses.

New and better Entrepreneurs who are involved with and committed to applying and valuing the **Odebrecht Hallmark:**

a Large Firm with the spirit of a Small Firm,

which is **light, agile, lean** and **flexible** and focused on satisfying **each Client's specific needs** with a **modest, unassuming** attitude.

In light of the stage attained by the Odebrecht Group, its **growth strategy** must be enriched with a new focus:

the difference between investment administration and business administration.

This difference requires an explanation.

When I began my entrepreneurial career, I was clearly aware that the **results** of the **businesses** I led had a definite purpose: paying the principal and interest on the **debts** that Emílio

Odebrecht & Cia. had been obliged to take on due to the adverse circumstances caused by World War II.

When these debts had been paid, a **positive cash balance** began to appear, and I realized that rather than belonging to me, this balance belonged to the present and future **Shareholders** of Construtora Norberto Odebrecht S.A.

It became clear that a dual role was necessary: interesting myself in the **businesses' results** and, at the same time, becoming interested in **return on investment.**

This dual role troubled me for several years, and led me to make bad investments that resulted in significant capital losses.

Once I had regained the capacity to invest in what was by then CNO, I only managed to overcome the **investor** vs. **entrepreneur** dichotomy some time later, through the creation of the holding company Odebrecht S.A.

Summarizing this learning experience:

- **business administration,** which emphasizes **results**, has to do with the **Client's satisfaction;** and

- **investment administration,** which emphasizes returns made up of the **results** that flow from the Operational Area, is oriented towards the **Shareholders' satisfaction** and takes place within Odebrecht S.A. through permanent interaction between the people Responsible for Business Areas and the Board of Directors.

The **synergetic** and **productive integration** of the Client's and Shareholders' satisfaction is the healthiest way of ensuring the Odebrecht Group's **growth** and **perpetuity.**

This integration requires a constant search for **dialogue, negotiation** and **agreement** among the people who **administer investments** and those who **administer** the Group's **businesses.** In the course of this process, each person must play his role and everyone must be imbued with **team spirit.**

. . .

This third edition resulted from the joint efforts of the author and the Members of a Committee specifically created to work with Emílio Odebrecht on the revision of ***Survival, Growth and Perpetuity.***

The Committee Members included, in alphabetical order:

Álvaro Cunha,
Gilberto Sá,
João Paiva Chaves,
Renato Baiardi,
Sergio Foguel and
Victor Gradin.

I would like to thank each of these long-standing Fellow Members for the opportunity to engage in rewarding team work, their spirit of contribution and creativity, as well as their disciplined investment of time and energy.

I would also like to extend my thanks to Antônio Carlos Viard, who has helped me with the writing of this book since the first edition.

. . .

At the time of this edition's publication, we are living – fully – in the **Age of Knowledge.**

In this era, Tangible Assets represented by **fixed capital investments** are no longer decisive.

What are decisive, today and in the future, are **Intangible Assets** made up of the organization's **culture** and **image**, as well as the **virtues, knowledge, expertise** and **skills** of **effective** and **contributive Leaders** and **Teams** who are **mature** enough to transform their **intelligence** into the **services** and **goods** the Client **wants** and **needs.**

Therefore, Odebrecht's greatest challenge is structuring itself as an **Organization of Knowledgeable People** for whom "international operations" will be merely a consequence of winning over **unique Client**s who are visualized in the context of their **respective Communities** and completely **satisfied.**

This **Organization of Knowledgeable People** must be capable of continuously **reinventing** and **renewing** itself through **creativity, innovation** and **team spirit.**

Thanks to the work of **creative** and **innovative Knowledgeable People**, it will be possible to identify **trends**, outline **scenarios,** reconceive **Businesses** and thereby keep the Group **permanently up to date** and abreast of **present** and **future challenges**.

For all these reasons, I believe that

> ***building an Organization of Knowledgeable People dedicated to the Client's satisfaction***

must be the mission of People in their First, Second and Third Ages who make up the Odebrecht Group wherever in the world their **spirit of service** may lead them.

It must be made clear that the **social responsibility** of the Group's Members consists of promoting the **continuous production of moral** and **material wealth,** for the benefit of the Client, Users and the Communities in which they work, as well as Shareholders and themselves.

This can only take place to the extent that they ensure **productivity, liquidity** and **image** and the Group's consequent **profitability**; in other words, its **survival**.

Once **survival** is assured, it will be possible to bring about **healthy growth**; this means **organic, harmonious** and **balanced** growth achieved through the **continuous reinvestment** of the net **results** available in cash, and the **integration** of **successive generations** of **new** and **better Entrepreneurs**.

These successive generations will keep the Group on the path towards **perpetuity**.

As we can see,

> *survival, growth and perpetuity are the watchwords for the Odebrecht Group's Members when fulfilling their social responsibility in practice.*

. . .

In *Pontos de Referência*, which was published in 1970, I wrote that the art of **leadership** can be **learned**.

In order for the present and potential **Leaders** of **Small Firms** and their Team Members to practice this art well, they must **master** and **apply** the **Odebrecht Entrepreneurial Technology (TEO)**.

Mastering and **applying TEO** in order to continually add value to the **Odebrecht Hallmark** requires the identification of

■ what **has been significant** (original, important, meaningful) in Odebrecht's past life;

■ and what must be **developed** and **maintained** to **build, ensure** and **improve** its **Future**.

The following have been and **will continue to be significant**:

■ the **universality** of the Odebrecht Group's **Philosophical Concepts**, which permits the Group's Entrepreneurs to apply them locally when serving their Clients in Communities with vastly different cultures;

- the **spirit of service** and **enthusiasm** transmitted through these **Philosophical Concepts;**

- the vision of **how to win over, maintain** and **increase** the **loyalty** of these **Clients** through the continuous practice of the **humility** and **simplicity** that characterize **Odebrecht's Hallmark;**

- the **creativity** and **innovation** needed to build up entrepreneurial structures (Teams) that are lean, flexible and tailored for **each Client,** who must be won over and maintained by being **increasingly satisfied;**

- the concern of the **Small Firm's Leader** and his **Team,** as well as the **Large Firm's Leader** and **Educator,** regarding **survival**, without which **growth is impossible;**

- the concern with focusing **simultaneously on growth** and **perpetuity** by grooming and integrating new Generations of better Entrepreneurs;

- considering the **Client** and **Shareholder** to be the Group Companies' **sources of life,** which must be simultaneously satisfied by its Entrepreneurs from the basis of frank, honest and trustworthy dialogue and negotiations;

- the **federative** and **confederate ties** that unify the Group and enable it to offer Clients and Shareholders the **best** the **Small** and **Large Firm** have to offer **simultaneously;**

■ dynamic decisionmaking and actions that make it necessary to **unlearn** in order to **learn new lessons;**

■ **decentralization** and **partnership,** which make it necessary to have Entrepreneur-Partners who have mastered and apply TEO, think in the long term, and are **committed to Odebrecht's Mission** and **Philosophical Concepts;**

■ the permanent development of **TEO** through the **exchange of knowledge** and **information,** as well as mastery of new **communication** and **information technologies** that help confer **cultural unity** on the Odebrecht Group's Teams wherever their Clients require their presence (anywhere in the world).

For all these reasons, we can conclude that in order for Odebrecht **to survive, grow** and **perpetuate** itself, it must **identify,** help **develop** and immediately **integrate ever-better Entrepreneurs** and **Support.**

Salvador, 20 March 1998

Norberto Odebrecht

Philosophical Concepts

Now and **always**, the Shareholders want the Odebrecht Group to be administered by **Knowledgeable People** with whom they share the same **Philosophical Concepts** and **entrepreneurial aims.**

As we shall see in the course of this book, these Philosophical Concepts and aims have distinguished Odebrecht as an **outstanding organization** in and of the **businesses** and **regions** in which it is present.

Within the Odebrecht Group, each Client must have an Entrepreneur at their disposal who is directly committed to their satisfaction and with whom they can communicate directly through frank, honest and trustworthy dialogue.

When serving **his** Client, this Entrepreneur is responsible for coordinating and integrating the knowledge of a Team put together to suit that particular Client's needs. This Team must be organized dynamically as these needs develop, both in terms of **time** and **geography.**

The Knowledgeable People who make up the Group's Teams do not need "bosses." They require freely accepted Leaders who support each Individual's **development** through permanent **education through work.**

These Knowledgeable People must be imbued with the **spirit of service** and know how to exercise this **spirit** in the Client's interests, from the basis of mutual **discipline, respect** and **friendship**, as well as **loyalty** to the Group.

To do so, they must creatively apply their **Philosophical Concepts**, no matter where they may be working, and be prepared to provide service with the **modest** and **unassuming** attitude the Client desires.

The **Fundamental Principles** and **Basic Tenets** presented here constitute the **essence** of the Odebrecht Group's Philosophical Concepts.

It is the **right** and **duty** of every Member of the Group to grasp, accept and apply the subject matter presented in the first two chapters of this book.

Through the disciplined application of these principles and tenets, the Group's Members can make their **qualities productive** while **focusing** on **contribution, opportunities** and **results** in light of the Client and their satisfaction, as well as their own **development** as Human Beings and Entrepreneurs.

PART I

Philosophical Concepts

CHAPTER 1

Fundamental Principles

T he **principles** presented here comprise the **basis** of the **cultural** and **ethical touchstones** for business management within the Odebrecht Group.

It is the duty of all the Group's Members to be the **Keepers** of these **principles,** because they constitute the **essence** of the Shareholders' **Intangible Assets.**

These cultural and ethical touchstones are in no way a "**straight-jacket**" designed to restrain the **initiative, creativity** and **style** of the Human Beings who freely accept and apply them.

On the contrary, they are aimed at **empowering** the Individual's ability to **make things happen** and enabling Human Beings to make their **personal mark** on the **facts** and **acts** of entrepreneurial life.

These principles have to do with:
the Individual;
Communication;
Synergy;
Creativity;
Partnership;
Productivity;
Education through Work; and
Reinvestment.

1. THE INDIVIDUAL

Confidence in the Individual's **potential** and **desire** to **progress** is the **basis** for the Odebrecht Group's **Philosophical Concepts.**

Human Beings are the **beginning** and **end** of all of society's actions, and their work is the essential means of achieving the **survival**, **growth** and **perpetuity** of humankind.

Work should be both a **duty** and a **right**, because the Individual **frees** and **humanizes** himself through productive labor.

Work is an inseparable part of the Human Character as a whole, which must be respected in every aspect of its nature.

Every Human Being has

- a **personality** and specific **needs** which he aspires to fulfill; and

- **control** over the **quality** and **productivity** of his performance.

The Individual's noblest deed is

serving his fellow Human Beings.

Only those people who accept and apply this supreme value will successfully integrate themselves into the Odebrecht Group.

The Individual's most important **asset** is his **spirit**, because this is what confers **character** and the **desire to serve**, as well as the

strength to create, innovate and **produce** for the benefit of his fellow Human Beings.

Within the Company, rather than having a "boss," the Individual requires a freely accepted Leader whose job is to coordinate and integrate his Team Members' work.

It is the Leader's duty to identify the **character, desire to serve** and **strengths** of each Team Member in order to encourage the Individual's **development** and increase his contribution to the production of **more** and **better wealth.**

To become productive, the Individual needs **motivation, encouragement** and the opportunity – received from his Leader – to achieve professional and financial fulfillment, as well as an Action Program defined through **dialogue, negotiation** and **agreement** between Leader and Team Member.

Only those **Leaders** who are aware of this responsibility can

- create a **favorable climate** for productive work that enriches the Individual, the Company and the Community; and

- reach an agreement with each Team Member on how they will **share** the **wealth** they helped create through the **interaction** between **their strengths** and those of the Group.

To varying degrees, everyone within a Company must have a **coordinating** and **integrating** vision in order to understand how they can each make a **contribution,** thereby helping increase the **effectiveness** and **efficiency** of their **joint efforts.**

It is the Leader's task to create and improve the **motivation** that heightens each Team Member's **awareness** of his personal **responsibility** for the **results** of his work.

As for the Team Member, he is responsible for

- contributing to his own **development** as well as that of the other Human Beings with whom he interacts;

- planning and executing work that is done well (efficiency) and on time (effectiveness); and

- committing himself to the constant search for **productivity** and the other **results** which this entails.

In light of these beliefs and values regarding the Individual in general, a detailed examination of the **beliefs** and **values** that constitute the essence of the **Odebrecht Entrepreneurial Technology** is in order regarding the Individual's roles as

Client, Entrepreneur and Shareholder.

1.1. *THE CLIENT*

The idea that the Individual is entirely self-sufficient is pure fiction. In the real world, the production of wealth imposes several forms of **interdependence** with his fellow Human Beings on every Individual.

The **division of labor** requires that everyone cooperate in pursuit of a **common goal.**

It also requires that they **give service first** in order to **receive service later on,** because the goods and services they produce are only transformed into **wealth** when they have been **sold, billed** and **paid for.**

The Individual ensures his survival by contributing to the survival of his fellow Human Beings. Similarly, the Company can only **survive** by **ensuring its Clients' satisfaction.**

Furthermore, to bring about its **healthy growth** and thereby **perpetuate** itself, the Odebrecht Group (through its Entrepreneurs) must continuously **identify new Clients, win them over** and immediately transform each of them into a **Satisfied Client.**

It can be said that

> *the Client's Satisfaction is the basis for the Odebrecht Group's existence.*

A warning is in order here: the Client is always **one** Person or a perfectly **individualized group** of People who are capable of **deciding** whether the services and goods produced represent **effective wealth** in their eyes.

It is a dangerous abstraction to view one's Clients as generic, impersonal organizations, because this can make one lose sight of the **Individual** who **follows up on, appraises and judges** the services and goods being provided and offers fair **compensation** in exchange.

The understanding that a **Company** is a **living social organism** arises from the realization that

■ the wealth it generates is destined for Human Beings and

■ it is created and directed by Human Beings.

Therefore, it is naïve to speak of abstract "market forces" to which Companies must adapt.

"Markets" arise from continuous **entrepreneurial action,** because the aim of each specific business must always be

the Client's satisfaction.

What the **demanding Client wants** and **needs**; what this Client considers **valuable**: these are the **decisive** factors which provide jobs and therefore the basis upon which the Entrepreneur can **plan**.

> *The Odebrecht Group Entrepreneur's business is to constantly exercise the right and duty to serve his Client. It always has been and always will be.*

This is the **essence** of the Business of each of the Odebrecht Group's Entrepreneurs.

It is vital that this **understanding** be **shared** by our present Leaders, those who are being groomed for leadership, and each and every Member of the Group.

1.2. *The Entrepreneur*

"**Client**" and "**Entrepreneur**" are highly **concrete** terms; there is nothing "abstract" about them.

Relations with **individual** Clients presuppose the commitment of a clearly **individualized Entrepreneur** who is responsible for managing the Group's business with a specific Client.

It must be deeply rooted in the mind of every active or emerging Entrepreneur that he can only exercise the **power to serve** when

- the Shareholders' Philosophical Concepts, applied in practice, take the form of **winning over** and **satisfying** the Client; and

- the Client's satisfaction is converted into **results** for the Shareholders.

In light of his commitment to serving his Client, the Entrepreneur must always be **modest** and **unassuming.**

In light of his commitment to the Client's satisfaction, it is essential for the Entrepreneur to make his business **better** rather than merely making it **bigger.**

The Entrepreneur is **appraised** on the basis of the results he achieves when working with the Team he leads. And this **appraisal** is the basis upon which his Leader must **judge** this Entrepreneur's performance.

The value of the services and goods provided will grow to the same extent that each Entrepreneur attains a **mastery** of his respective business.

Such **mastery**, in turn, arises from the successful identification of the Client's **needs** and **expectations** with a view to ensuring their **satisfaction**.

1.2.1. *Focusing on Contributions, Opportunities and Results*

An Entrepreneur is a person whose aim in life is serving his Client. To do so, he directs the production of moral and material wealth by **coordinating** other Human Beings who are experts in specific technologies and **integrating** the results of their respective tasks while keeping to a previously established **schedule** and **budget**.

The Entrepreneur has a basic commitment to exercising his **expertise** in order to make his and his Team Members' **knowledge productive** while focusing on **contributions, opportunities** and **results**.

The people comprising the Entrepreneur's Team must align themselves with this basic commitment so that their **contributions** are focused on identifying **opportunities** and producing **results**.

1.2.2. *Entrepreneurial Spirit*

The entrepreneurial spirit consists of

- the Entrepreneur's **awareness** that his **mission** is to **give service**; and

- the **effective performance** of this mission by making his and his Team Members' strengths **productive** in conjunction with the **force** of **circumstance**.

Although it is a pre-requisite for possessing entrepreneurial spirit, just having the **spirit of service** alone is not enough.

The Individual who is endowed with **entrepreneurial spirit** must not only be willing to give of himself for the benefit of his fellow Human Beings but be committed to the permanent creation of improved and greater wealth on time and within budget in order to continue giving more and better service.

The **spirit of service** can only be transformed into **entrepreneurial spirit** when it is supplemented by the continuous **production of results**.

To **produce results** an Entrepreneur must be endowed with a number of **qualities**, including the **courage** to impose his own **decisions** and **priorities** on **time** and **events** with a view to improving his business.

1.2.3. *The Entrepreneur's Role in Society*

The Entrepreneur's **role in society** is explained and justified by his ability to coordinate and integrate the production of wealth to the extent that he continuously transforms his and his Team Members' **creativity** into **innovations** and these into ever **better** and **greater results.**

These results are produced to

- **compensate** the **Partners** who help produce the services and goods the Client wants;

- provide qualified and continuous **return** on the **Shareholders'** investment;

- generate increasingly **positive cash balances** to leverage new opportunities identified to serve their Clients and Communities, and thereby add value to the Shareholders' Assets; and

- create opportunities for Partners to work and **progress.**

Only when (and while) he has **control** over **time** and **events** can the Individual Responsible for Results fully assume his role as an Entrepreneur, because then he can mobilize the **strengths of Human Beings** and the **force of circumstance** to achieve his **priorities.**

> *Rather than contemplating the world, the Entrepreneur must change it.*

The **Entrepreneur** must be capable of appraising the **situation**, changing **existing economic conditions** and **innovating** by **creating new economic conditions**.

To do so, he must **concentrate** everyone's **energies** on what is, in fact, their **top priority: identifying, winning over** and **satisfying** the Client, **today, tomorrow** and **always**.

1.2.4. *Courage vs. Analysis*

The successful Entrepreneur always points to **whatever makes the difference** because **results** are his **reward** for making a **unique** (or at least **significant**) **contribution** that is recognized as such by his Client.

The Entrepreneur must analyze the situation before taking action. However, more than analysis, it is the **courage to take action** that characterizes the Entrepreneur's **spirit** and leads to **success**.

In the business world, **success** arises from the right **choice** of priorities, a **focus** on these **priorities**, and above all the **impact** of the **decision** to transform such **priorities** into **results**.

That is why the Entrepreneur must always

- study **new ways** of giving **better service** to his Clients;

- recall the lessons he has learned while forgetting past events that are no longer productive, and focusing on the **future**; and

- choose his **own direction**.

The **spirit** that drives him makes the Entrepreneur insatiable in his quest to improve what already exists, because he is **never satisfied with the results achieved.**

Looking to the **future** rather than contemplating the **past**, and forgetting past events that have **ceased to be productive** is imperative for **survival**.

The Individual who delights in "past successes" relinquishes his standing as an Entrepreneur.

Those who focus on immediate results and prove incapable of **subordinating** the **present** to the **future** of their Company will also relinquish this standing.

It is essential for the Entrepreneur to be able to choose his **own direction** and refuse to follow others out of habit. To **successfully** manage a business in which **time** is **irretrievable** and **results are achieved,** the Entrepreneur will need

> *more courage than analysis; more impact than technique.*

More courage than analysis when identifying the **priorities** on which he must concentrate.

More impact than technique when making his **decision**.

1.2.5. *Problems vs. Opportunities*

Focusing more on **opportunities** than on **problems** means taking into account that obstacles and challenges confront the Entrepreneur as a **natural consequence** of his actions.

Problems can only be overcome through **further action** which transforms them into **opportunities** to give **better service**.

In addition to knowing what he wants, the Entrepreneur must be able to

- **seek out** different opinions;

- be sufficiently **humble** to integrate other arguments with his own ideas and, if necessary, reformulate or consolidate his opinion; and

- have the **courage** to abide by his **opinion** when convinced he is on the right path, even when confronted by opposing arguments.

> *Failing to make a decision at the right time is worse than making a wrong decision. It betrays a lack of entrepreneurial spirit.*

The Entrepreneur must have the **courage to decide** and **act at the right moment.**

An exaggerated "fear of making mistakes" can confuse and immobilize both the Leader and his Team Members.

The Entrepreneur's **courage** is a virtue that permits him to identify and quickly correct his errors, as well as enabling him to educate himself and his Team Members.

Anyone who wants to learn about a given subject in full detail before taking action will never make an **entrepreneurial decision.**

Entrepreneurial decisions must be simultaneously directed

- towards **effectiveness, to identify the right thing;** and

- towards **efficiency, to do the right thing well.**

Just as **decisionmaking** precedes the **process,** the quest for **effectiveness** must precede the search for **efficiency.**

1.2.6. *Discipline and Creativity*

To be oriented towards **effectiveness,** the Entrepreneur requires **self-discipline.**

It is through self-discipline that the Entrepreneur avoids dissipating his and his Team Members' strengths on things that are "superfluous," "useless" and even "harmful."

The orientation towards **efficiency** also requires **self-discipline** from the Entrepreneur and his Partners so that all can seek productivity:

> *better results achieved through more quality obtained in less time, at a lower cost.*

Self-discipline simultaneously contributes to effectiveness and efficiency, in addition to becoming a powerful weapon for overcoming the tendency towards **deterioration** that naturally establishes itself in a Company and must therefore be the target of systematic struggle.

For a Company not only to **survive** but **grow** and **perpetuate itself**, discipline must be accompanied by **creativity**.

To be creative, the Entrepreneur must be **open minded** and **free of prior conditioning** so that he can **influence others** and **be influenced** when seeking **what is right**.

The **synergetic** integration of **creativity** and **discipline** through **useful** and **productive innovations** that create the satisfied Client and win their respect for the Entrepreneur is beyond the scope of conventional "bosses." **It is essential to have a Leader**.

1.2.7. *Leadership*

"Subordination" is foreign to the principle of **leadership,** which must be freely accepted rather than "imposed."

In an organization based on leadership, there is no such thing as "hierarchical levels" and much less "vertical organization charts." Strictly speaking, it contains **spheres of operations** and **horizontal structures.**

Leadership is the ability to motivate other Human Beings to work towards the Company's **objectives** and **priorities** by guiding Team Members to attain ever-higher targets and encouraging the transformation of those who have the **potential** and **will** into **new** and **better Entrepreneurs.**

A Leader creates and strengthens **confidence** among Human Beings who have **freely** decided to share the same Philosophical Concepts and make their best contribution in order to achieve common aims.

Rather than accepting what already exists, the Leader must constantly **study** and apply **innovations** that make **Human Beings' strengths** and the **force of circumstance** more productive to obtain more and better results.

An **Individual** becomes a **Leader** when he focuses on the **strengths** and **contributions** of his fellow Human Beings in practice.

A Leader is always looking for answers to the question that he constantly asks himself when dealing with each of his Team Members:

> ***"What is it that this Individual can do extraordinarily well and could do even better?"***

By proceeding this way, the Leader reiterates his confidence in People, respects their individual characteristics and creates conditions that enable each Team Member to develop his potential.

> ***Part of the Leader's wisdom includes detailed, in-depth knowledge of the People with whom he works.***

Due to his realism, the Leader knows that it is unrealistic to wait for "ideal" Human Beings to appear.

If an Individual who is duly aligned with the Group's Philosophical Concepts is also an expert in a specific technology that is indispensable to the satisfaction of a given Client and knows how to convert his knowledge into the expected results, the Leader must accept this Human Being and motivate him to achieve **success.**

To best direct the Human Beings who accept his leadership, the Leader must always

- use dialogue as the primary tool for action to get to know each Team Member's strengths, enable the Team Member to get to know him and thereby consolidate a relationship of mutual trust;

- encourage his own creativity and that of his Team Members with a view to ensuring the organization's survival, growth and perpetuity; and

- play an educational role that cannot be delegated, by helping groom other Leaders capable of becoming even better Entrepreneurs than he is.

A strong leader identifies and helps groom strong Leaders who are prepared to overcome the tendency towards **deterioration** and lead the Company to new heights of **organic, healthy growth.**

Regarding the Leader's educational role, we must be clearly aware that

> *the measure of a Leader's quality is the quality of his Team Members.*

A true Leader

- **influences** and is **influenced** by his Team Members during the pursuit of **what is right;**

- wins over his Team Members so that they freely adhere to the Shareholders' **aims** and seek to achieve those aims in full alignment with the Leader; and

- acts as an **educator** because he finds the greatest personal and professional fulfillment in the grooming of **new Leaders.**

The sign of a true Leader is his ability to transcend his own individuality; to consider the grooming of Human Beings whom he has helped integrate into the Group the **most splendid monument** that could perpetuate his memory.

> *Identifying, grooming and integrating new and better entrepreneurs in the hard school of productivity is the noblest aspect of the entrepreneurial task.*

A Leader is capable of

- instilling **discipline** in his Team Members and winning their **respect** to bring about the Company's **healthy growth;**

- generating a relationship of **confidence** and **friendship** with his Team Members as well as among them while creating opportunities for all to **progress** simultaneously; and

- creating a climate of **loyalty** to the Philosophical Concepts and aims of his Company, which is essential to its **perpetuity** and the personal and professional fulfillment of this generation and the next.

1.3. *Shareholders*

These are Human Beings endowed with the **spirit of service** who have placed their **Intangible** and **Tangible Assets** at the Company's disposal.

The Shareholders' Intangible Assets consist of their **Beliefs** and **Values** and the **Aims** they believe to be the best suited to satisfying the Company's Clients and their own expectations, as well as the **image** of the Group that is held by its Clients, the Community and Public Opinion in general.

This is why the true starting point for an adequately structured Company is the Shareholders' **Intangible Assets.**

The Entrepreneur must convert the Shareholders' Beliefs and Values, as well as their Aims, into what is truly fundamental: **the Client's satisfaction**.

Figure 1.1 shows that the Shareholders' **spirit of service flows** towards the Client.

Figure 1.2. depicts the role of the Entrepreneur, which is to ensure that **results flow back** from the Client in the direction of the Shareholders, and therefore create the conditions for his Company's **healthy** and **continuous growth.**

To better establish this idea, I should stress the meaning of **entrepreneurial spirit.**

Entrepreneurial spirit ensures that the Shareholders' **spirit of service flows towards** the Client, generates **team spirit** among Team Members and consequently ensures that **more** and **better results** than those **agreed** upon **flow back** in return.

Transforming the Spirit of Service into Results

1.1. FLUX

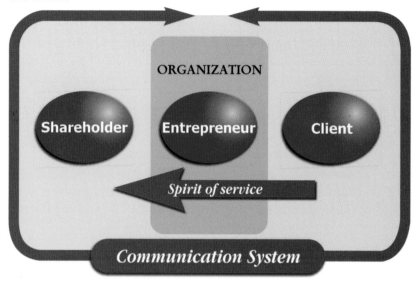

1.2. REFLUX

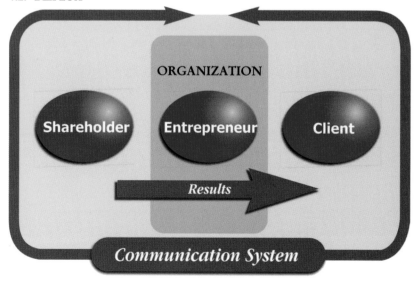

By permanently establishing and heightening the **interaction** between **Shareholders** and the **Client**, the Entrepreneur **explains** and **justifies** his role as well as the compensation he deserves.

The Community needs **constantly growing** businesses that focus on the Individual's development, transform his work into **effective wealth** and promote his **physical** and **mental health**.

In their turn,

> *Shareholders are satisfied by adequate return on investment and the safe appreciation of the Intangible and Tangible Assets they have entrusted to the Entrepreneur.*

Return on investment and the **appreciation** of the Shareholders' Assets are **natural consequences** of the fair and adequate application of the Odebrecht Entrepreneurial Technology to the entrepreneurial task of **identifying**, **winning over** and **satisfying** the Client with whom a **lasting relationship** has been established.

2. COMMUNICATION

It is an unquestionable fact that **interdependence** presupposes **free communication** between Human Beings.

To communicate is to share the knowledge, information and **desires** which Human Beings require to create wealth.

To communicate is also to create a **two-way** channel between equally **free** Human Beings by encouraging each Individual to interact with others, as long as he is willing to **influence** and **be influenced** in the search for **what is right** for everyone.

The Entrepreneur who is a **true leader** recognizes that Human Beings have the right to make **free** and **informed choices.** He is therefore responsible for creating the conditions for enabling them each individually to **grasp, understand, accept** and **apply** the Shareholders' **Philosophical Concepts.**

Then, in order to put these Concepts into practice, he **motivates, coordinates** and **integrates** his Team Members through the **spoken word.**

The **written word** and the **language of numbers,** although valuable communication tools, must only be used to supplement **direct verbal Person-to-Person contact.**

Providing, obtaining and utilizing **adequate information** at the **right time,** knowing how to listen to or read Team Members' opinions and precisely communicate his thoughts, either verbally or in writing, are **innate** or **acquired skills** that an Entrepreneur must constantly improve in order to be **successful.**

> *The Leader's authority is conferred on him by his Team Members.*

This is why the Entrepreneur must be eloquent in order to **captivate** his Partners and induce them to choose the **right thing** and do it well.

This means leading them freely to apply the Shareholders' Philosophical Concepts and thereby avoid wasting **time, energy** and **money** on useless debate regarding "who is right and who is wrong."

The drive to captivate his Partners requires that the Entrepreneur be **forceful** in order to overcome his **weaknesses** and make even more productive the **strengths** of those people who, of their own free will, have decided to become his Team Members and are willing to cultivate **discipline** and **respect** and, through them, consolidate **mutual trust**.

> *In the age of knowledge, the complacent will be constantly pushed aside by new ideas, new methods, new technologies and the aggressiveness of the next generations.*

Life is a **challenge**, and this is even more true for the Entrepreneur.

For him, living means understanding the **trends** that arise in **each present situation** and anticipating them with a view to building the **future situation he desires**.

It is naïve to think that a Leader can obstruct the progress of events or bend them to his will.

Those who attempt to use the **present** to subjugate the **future** to the **past** are doomed to failure.

> *The future serves itself, and it is the Leader's job to become its servant.*

The best tool available to help Human Beings anticipate the course of events is a **Company** conceived and directed from the basis of a **strategy,** both of which can be improved over time.

Conceiving a Company and its strategy is more than just a "technical" task; it is a **political-strategic task** which the Entrepreneur cannot and must not delegate.

Before being a **planner,** the **Entrepreneur** must be a **pragmatic strategist** who is **skilled** in interpersonal relations.

Only the Entrepreneur who has a complete mastery of the Odebrecht Entrepreneurial Technology will know how to organize the work of his Team Members and integrate the specific technologies for which they have expertise to obtain the results the Client and Shareholders want and need.

There is nothing complicated about organization; it is very simple, as long as the Entrepreneur is aware of a basic truth:

> *the only forces that effectively exist within an organization are Leaders and their teams, their respective businesses and the communication between them; everything else is a consequence of these forces.*

Acceptance of this basic truth will simplify the task of organization. The Entrepreneur's challenge is to choose the Human Beings with whom he will manage his **Company** and conduct his **strategy** with a view to producing more and better wealth.

Once these Human Beings have been chosen and the strategy outlined, he must create and establish a **Communication System** that involves the Entrepreneur himself, his Team Members, the Client and the Shareholder, as suggested in Figure 1.3.

When thus created and established, the **Communication System** will make it possible for the **follow-up, appraisal** and **judgment** of **results** to become a task shared by everyone involved.

The three figures shown here so far can be combined into one.

Figure 1.4 illustrates how the **spirit of service flows out** and the **results flow back,** as well as the **Communication System** involving the **Client,** the **Entrepreneur,** his **Team Members** and the **Shareholders.**

3. SYNERGY

Where there is **communication,** there will be **dialogue, negotiation** and **agreement** among Leaders, their Team Members, the other Economic Agents involved and the Client regarding the **expected results.**

It will also create a **climate** in which the Economic Agents feel that they are Partners and the Entrepreneur can motivate everyone to seek **common results.**

The paradigm for this should be the following truth:

1.3.

> # HUMAN BEINGS ORGANIZED AND INTEGRATED AS A TEAM, AND THEIR BUSINESS
>
> ### *Communication*

1.4.

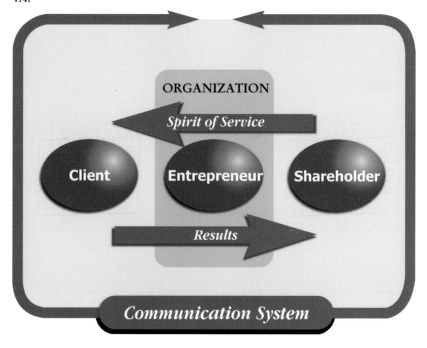

Human Beings are unified by the production of moral and material wealth.

Synergy, when applied to human society, means the **coordinated** and **integrated actions** of Human Beings seeking to energize **shared results**.

As experience has shown, where there is effective synergy, the **simultaneous actions** of Human Beings working together will produce **greater results** than those obtained through the sum of their individual actions.

The Entrepreneur will only truly lead when he coordinates and integrates the simultaneous actions of Human Beings so that they can produce more wealth together than each could produce individually.

Building and increasing People's **synergy** is the Entrepreneur's **priority mission** when working with his Partners. Synergy makes it possible to

- continuously create a **whole that is greater than the sum of its parts**;

- maintain solid ties of **discipline, respect** and **friendship** among Partners; and

- strengthen everyone's **mutual trust** and **loyalty** to the Company.

4. CREATIVITY

Through the constant exercise of **creativity,** the **synergy** between Human Beings leads to the production of **greater** and **better wealth.**

The Entrepreneur's creativity must be based on **concrete reality.**

The true Entrepreneur always works from the basis of his Client's **needs** to stimulate his creativity.

It is when dealing with specific issues and, above all, in the course of **communication** that the Entrepreneur questions and confronts his reality by **disciplining** his own **creativity** and that of his Team Members in the search for **productive** and **useful innovations** for their Client.

An innovation can be **generalized** with the aim of applying it in different areas from that in which it originated. However, once opportunities to apply it have been identified, they must immediately turn from the general to the specific so that this innovation can be successfully put into practice.

The final aim of any **innovation policy** can only have one starting point – the Client's **needs** – and one ultimate goal – their **satisfaction.**

Rather than waiting for an opportunity to "arise" or "appear," the Entrepreneur and his Team must actively seek it, primarily

outside the Company, because that is where they will find the opportunities that produce results.

In addition to identifying **new opportunities**, the Entrepreneur must be creative when perceiving that **old ways** of **serving** and **acting** are becoming outdated and replace them before they deteriorate.

Because ideas must be **accepted** rather than "imposed," those who seek to realize opportunities before the Client sufficiently appreciates them will squander their creativity.

The Entrepreneur's **commitment** to the **real** and **concrete** is the permanent touchstone for his creative efforts and, therefore,

> *a creative idea is only an entrepreneurial idea when it can be converted into an opportunity to give better service.*

The transformation of an **opportunity** into a **business** and that business into **results** requires the continuous intervention of **creativity** to **effectively** and **efficiently** carry out the **entrepreneurial task** of satisfying the Client.

Creativity is inseparable from the **entrepreneurial spirit**, which will wither and die if satisfaction with "past successes" diminishes the Entrepreneur's creativity.

The Entrepreneur is committed to **making things happen**; to a **future** which is **always one step ahead**.

People endowed with the true entrepreneurial spirit are constantly **dissatisfied** with recently achieved results, which drives them to continuously study new ways of using their creativity to **improve those results.**

It is futile and dangerous to believe that "if things are going well, they should be left the way they are."

In the real world, those who think everything is going just fine are failing to do something that is **fundamental** to **improving the results even further.**

5. PARTNERSHIP

Partnership is a **moral** and **psychological contract** between Leader and Team Member through which each is committed to the success of their joint enterprise.

It is a dangerous simplification to believe that **partnership** means sharing results.

Partnership requires the Individual's **involvement** both in the **planning** and **execution** of the **Entrepreneurial Task**; that is, from the time the Client is **won over** to the time they are **satisfied.**

Partnership requires **commitment** to obtaining **productivity** and everything it entails, with a view to **surpassing** the **results agreed upon** by the Partners and therefore the **amount** to be **shared.**

In a partnership agreement, the Team Member

- seeks his own **development,** in harmony with the **growth** of the Company;

- has the opportunity to prepare himself to take on **greater challenges;** and

- simultaneously increases his **income** and **well-being.**

In his turn, the Leader seeks to ensure the **survival, growth** and **perpetuity** of his organization when creating the conditions for

- obtaining **productivity** and the resulting **profitability,** as well as **liquidity** and **image;**

- making **growing cash balances** available to compensate the Shareholders and finance investments;

- grooming the Small Firm's current and potential Leaders by means of **education through work** so that they can take on greater responsibility in the future; and

- simultaneously satisfying his Client and Shareholders.

6. PRODUCTIVITY

Productivity is the **never-ending process** of **improving intangible** and **tangible results** with **higher quality** in **less time** and at a **lower cost**.

In addition to being a process, productivity must also be a **permanent attitude** for the Small Firm's Leader and his Team when seeking **the right thing** and doing it well.

Productivity can also be defined as the **continuously harvested fruits** of the Entrepreneur's **creativity** when it is used to increase his Company's **synergy**.

Productivity as a process, an attitude and continuously harvested fruits will enable the Odebrecht Group to produce greater and better wealth for the benefit of the following people:

- the Client;

- the Community to which they belong;

- the Small Firm's Leader and his Team;

- the Supplier and other Economic Agents; and

- the Shareholders.

Profits, profitability and other indicators used to gauge an organization's **performance** are **merely** a **consequence** of the **productivity** achieved by the Small Firms' Leaders and their Teams.

Outstanding results obtained through the force of circumstance are not enough for the person Responsible for the Small Firm, his Leader and Shareholders.

Productivity alone, and particularly that which is **hard won** within the Operational Area, are the real measures of the performance of a Small Firm's Leader and his Team.

Within the Company, if each Individual attains a **mastery** over his business's productivity, there will be no barriers to **making things happen**, as well as to pursuing and achieving several different results at once.

The exclusive pursuit of short-term results tends to endanger the basis of the business, which is **serving the Client.**

Long-term vision is indispensable for generating **intangible results** such as **image** and the **integration** of **new** and **better** Entrepreneurs.

Once the **intangible** and/or **tangible results** to be achieved have been identified, it is essential to define the **standards** for **appraisal**, including **schedules** and **costs**.

In the case of tangible results, we must bear in mind that

only qualified, quantified and appraised results are meaningful. Results that fall outside this process are also excluded from the decisions and responsibilities of Human Beings, because they will eventually be forgotten.

A similar procedure must be followed for intangible results through the selection of suitable indicators.

7. EDUCATION THROUGH WORK

Within the Odebrecht Group, the Individual endowed with **potential** and the **desire to progress** must

- understand and accept the Group's Philosophical Concepts;

- effectively apply these Concepts when carrying out his Entrepreneurial Task on a daily basis in order to ensure that the Client is truly satisfied; and

- prepare himself to take on increasing responsibility that will enable him to equal or even surpass his Leader.

The aim of **education through work** is the **joint development** of Leader and Team Member and requires that both be **humble** and engage in honest, frank and trustworthy dialogue.

Another quality that is inseparable from their joint development is their mutual desire and ability to **unlearn** what is no longer productive and **learn** what can be useful in order to better satisfy the Client and Shareholders.

7.1. *Understanding And Accepting The Philosophical Concepts*

Giving service, being humble and unassuming, making work a source of pleasure and giving up the superfluous entail decisions that are very difficult to make and even harder to adhere to.

To be successful in the entrepreneurial life, the Individual who wants to become an Entrepreneur must share the beliefs and values inherent to those who are committed to producing wealth and following a code of ethics derived from those beliefs and values.

Even when he has been brought up to realize that his business is to serve, the Team Member will require his Leader's **time, presence, experience** and **example** to learn to serve his Client and exercise leadership in light of the realities and circumstances of the entrepreneurial life.

7.2. *Applying The Odebrecht Entrepreneurial Technology*

The Individual learns how to be an Entrepreneur by working in the **Operational Area**, where the Client is effectively won over, Human Beings are led and **results** are obtained.

Each Leader must **help** the Team Member **apply** the principles, concepts and standards that he must assimilate when doing his job on a **daily basis**.

The Leader is also responsible for **following up on** and **appraising** the Team Member to **judge** whether he has what it takes to progress as an Entrepreneur.

> *The Leader's task, which cannot be delegated, is to devote his time, presence, experience and example to the Team Member so that he can receive support, and his performance when applying lhe Odebrecht Entrepreneurial Technology can be followed up on, appraised and judged.*

This is the **essence** of the **Pedagogy of Presence,** the educational process through which the Leader seeks to groom **new** and **better** Entrepreneurs by continuously improving his Team Members and himself.

All of the Group Companies must be made up of increasingly mature and effective Leaders and Teams so the Client and Shareholders can benefit from the advantages of the **Odebrecht Hallmark**:

> *a Large Firm with the Spirit of a Small Firm.*

7.3. *MEETING THE CHALLENGE OF EXCELLING*

In a climate of mutual **trust** and **respect**, the Leader must love his Team Member as he would his own child, always remembering that, rather than protecting their children, Parents should prepare them to confront and overcome the hardships of life.

The Leader must present his Team Member with **successive challenges** that should always be **compatible** with the level of **maturity** he has attained. At the same time, the Team Member is responsible for seeking out such challenges.

It is essential for the Team Member to overcome these challenges on a **daily basis** and in **practice** in order to become an Entrepreneur and develop his ability to provide effective support with entrepreneurial spirit.

To the extent that he successfully takes on these challenges and excels, the Team Member can

- continue to promote his **self-development** while developing the potential of the People he will lead;

- complete his **education** as an Entrepreneur and, thanks to his Leader's help, become **even better** than that Leader.

If the Odebrecht Group's Leaders **surpass themselves** by grooming **ever-better Leaders,** the organization will be able to **grow** in an **organic** and **continuous** fashion.

8. REINVESTMENT

The formation and appreciation of **Intangible** and **Tangible Assets** is the basis for **social wealth.**

This is a **cumulative** process that only produces results when constant attention is paid to **balanced** and **safe reinvestment.**

Permanent reinvestment carried out in a **safe** and **balanced** fashion generates work opportunities and more and better wealth for the Community, as well as creating stronger, more dynamic Companies.

Reinvestment has been a constant factor in the life of the Odebrecht Group since its beginnings, in light of its commitment to **perpetuity.**

An inherent part of Odebrecht's culture is the conviction that the results obtained must be **concentrated** and **reinvested** with a view to **growing** the Group and consequently **adding value** to the Shareholders' Assets.

Philosophical Concepts

CHAPTER 2
Basic Tenets

T ogether with the fundamental principles discussed in the previous chapter, the basic tenets presented here constitute the **basis** for a **common language** and therefore the **Communication System** of the Odebrecht Group.

The aim of these tenets is to make the interaction between Leaders and their Team Members **effective**, because they require **intellectual discipline** from the Interlocutors while offering **clear communication** in exchange.

They are also the basis for the **efficiency** of their common language, as each tenet summarizes beliefs and values that need no repetition.

Five major groups of concepts will be examined in this chapter, in the following order:

Decentralization;
Planned delegation;
The entrepreneurial task;
Results; and
The Company's social responsibility.

1. DECENTRALIZATION

Decentralization is a **concept** that the Odebrecht Group has applied since its inception to carry out its **strategy** of **healthy, balanced** and **continuous growth.**

This **strategy** favors constant and direct contact with the Client, a clear perception of their needs and the best way of serving them, and the permanent integration of **new** and **better Entrepreneurs,** each at the head of his own **Team,** and focused on satisfying their respective Client.

In a **decentralized organization,** each Team Member must view his problems as **challenges** and transform them into **opportunities** to give **better service** and get **better results.**

Problems that can and must be solved by the Leader should not be passed on to his Team Members. The Leader should only communicate **solutions** to Team Members, expressing them in terms of **opportunities** and **results.**

Decisionmaking within the Odebrecht Group must also be done **individually,** because each Entrepreneur must be the **only person responsible** for making decisions in his sphere of operations.

It must be clearly understood that

responsibility cannot be delegated.

When delegating **authority** to a Team Member, the Leader remains **responsible** for any decisions that Team Member might make.

1.1. *CLIENT → SHAREHOLDER LINE*

The **Client** and **Shareholders** are the true **sources of power** within any Company, because

- it is the Client who transforms the **resources** mobilized to satisfy them into **wealth** by paying the invoices presented; and

- Shareholders are the **owners** of **Intangible** and **Tangible Assets**.

In the case of **Intangible Assets**, these are represented by the effective application of **Philosophical Concepts**; by **image**, **entrepreneurial aims** and particularly the **Hallmark** that characterizes the company.

The Entrepreneur is responsible for creating **communication** between these two **sources of power** and **dynamically harmonizing** their interests through a **two-way channel** along which

- the Shareholders' **spirit of service flows** towards the Client; and

- **results flow back** from the Client to the Shareholders.

In the specific case of the Odebrecht Group, the Small Firm's Leader is the essential link in this two-way channel.

To strengthen the ties between the Client and Shareholders, once a Contract has been signed or a Production Order received from the Client, and the Team Member's Action Program has been approved by the Leader, the Team Member must already have **defined**, **created** and prepared himself to set up

- his **Results Centers**;

- his **Support Team**; and

- his **Communication System**.

1.2. RESULTS CENTER

To be **successful**, a Company must be organized around Results Centers rather than "cost centers."

Results Centers must be established according to the different kinds of services and products specified in the tender or production order which, when integrated, result in the **product** the Client wants and is willing to pay for.

The **basic cell** is the Results Center and the person **Responsible**: a **Knowledgeable Individual** endowed with **entrepreneurial spirit** who is an expert in the specific production technology for a given group of services and products that can be measured, billed and paid for by the Client.

The simple idea that a Knowledgeable Individual – together with his strengths, focus on contribution and Action Program – represents a Results Center is the basis from which the **present** and **future** Small Firm must be built.

Everything else that must be allocated to this basic cell arises from the involvement and commitment of the person Responsible for that unit to helping satisfy his Client.

The person Responsible for a Results Center must receive all the **support** he needs from his immediate Leader, and when appropriate, even more than he asks for in order to continuously increase his **productivity.**

1.3. *SUPPORT TEAM*

In order to achieve ever-higher levels of **productivity,** the Team Member must be able to rely on the continued guidance of his Leader.

With the aim of sharing his **time, presence, experience** and **example** with each of his Team Members, the Leader must be **dynamically organized** so that he is **always available** at the right time to **concentrate** on what **matters** and **makes the difference** to the Team Member's **success.**

Like his **time,** the Leader's **knowledge** is limited.

That is why Specialists and Technicians are both necessary and valuable. They must be mobilized according to the Client's specific needs, with the mission of giving the Leader **support** in order to energize his **strengths** and increase his **time.**

That is also why the term **Support Team** has been devised to designate the position which the people Responsible for Support must occupy in the **time** and **"geography"** of the Odebrecht Group:

alongside the line, without confusing the two.

Rather than being a "position," Support is the **desire to serve** with **entrepreneurial spirit** and a focus on **contribution, opportunities** and **results.**

The Entrepreneur and each of his Support Team Members work for the same Client; this Client is located **outside** the Group and must be **identified, won over** and **satisfied.**

As with Line Members, the people comprising the Support Team must always have the **courage to contribute** in order to win over and satisfy their Client.

The Support Team Members must be involved with and committed to the **success** of the Leader's **educational task.**

1.4. *COMMUNICATION SYSTEM*

Having organized the Results Centers that will serve the Client and formed his Support Team, the Small Firm's Leader must create, establish and operate his **Communication System.**

Through the **means of communication** represented by the Action Plan of the Large Firm's Leader, his own Action Program and the reports and accounts it contains, this system enables the Small Firm's Leader to

■ stay in direct and constant touch with the Client;

■ reach a consensus on the results to be obtained through dialogue, negotiation and agreement;

■ follow up on, appraise and judge the performance of his Team Members as well as his own, in conjunction with the Large Firm's Leader; and

■ amend and/or endorse the results to be obtained in accordance with the data, facts, acts and results already accomplished.

1.5. *SMALL FIRM*

Having established his Results Center, put together his Support Team and implemented his Communication System, the Small Firm's Leader will be prepared to satisfy his Client.

Within the Odebrecht Group, the **Small Firm** is a concept that has nothing to do with any legal connotations.

The Small Firm is a **living center of interests** that is capable of simultaneously promoting:

- the Client's satisfaction;

- the personal and professional fulfillment of the Human Being who leads it and those who make up his Team, whether they are Line or Support Members; and

- the production of results that contribute to the Group's **survival** in order to finance its **growth** on a solid foundation.

The Small Firm is the best **entryway** which the Group offers those who accept its invitation to join its ranks.

By working closely with the Client under the guidance of a **Leader** and **educator,** newcomers will find optimum conditions for developing their **spirit of service, team spirit** and **entrepreneurial spirit.**

During the constant search for **productivity, liquidity** and **image,** they learn how to work with the Client as well as to identify **opportunities** and transform them into **results.**

They become aware, through practice, that the **present** and **future vitality** of the Odebrecht Group depends upon **lean, agile** and **flexible Small Firms** that have adapted themselves to the Client's **needs** and are **linked** to the Large Firm as members of a **federation.**

The cost of this Large Firm must be minimal. The Large Firm's Leader must be rewarded in accordance with his **contribution** to **increasing** the Small Firm's **productivity.** From his portion of the results, he will deduct the share earned by his few and indispensable **Support** Team Members.

Neither the Client nor Shareholders must be burdened by the Large Firm's expenses.

On the contrary, they must benefit from the **Odebrecht Hallmark:**

a Large Firm with the spirit of a Small Firm.

When they begin their careers in a Results Centers, newcomers become used to working with a **modest**, **unassuming** attitude. They soon discover that their **future** depends exclusively on their own **performance,** which can lead them to positions of **increasing responsibility** and **simultaneous fulfillment.**

1.6. *LARGE FIRM*

This term is understood to mean the structure that is under the responsibility of a **mature Leader** who gives his Team Members support to help them satisfy their respective Clients. In return for giving his Team Members **effective support,** the

Leader will receive:

- the constant **innovation** of the Small Firms;

- **net results** in the Large Firm's Cash balance, which are indispensable for financing the organization's Growth; and

- **experienced Entrepreneurs**, each of whom has been suitably groomed and is ready to take on the leadership of the present and future Large Firms.

1.7. *MODULAR STRUCTURE*

Today, tomorrow and **always**, the module that characterizes the Hallmark of

a Large Firm with the spirit of a Small Firm

must be the **basis** for the **strategy** of ensuring the Odebrecht Group's **healthy** and **continued growth** for the benefit of the Client and Shareholders.

Each Client must have a previously identified Entrepreneur to serve them at the head of his own Team.

And, according to the individual characteristics of each Business, they must have an experienced leader capable of sharing his **time, presence, experience** and **example** with the Entrepreneurs under his responsibility.

Figure 2.1. illustrates how this **growth strategy** has worked since the Group's beginnings:

Small Firm → Large Firm → Business Area

2. PLANNED DELEGATION

Within the Odebrecht Group, the practice of **confidence in** people is synonymous with **planned delegation.**

Through **planned delegation** we can build up a **dynamic modular structure** that is entirely focused on satisfying each **Client's** individual **needs.**

Delegating a task to someone means having **confidence** in

■ the **rectitude** of his **character;**

■ the Individual's **potential** and **desire** to **progress;**

■ his **competence;** and

■ his **alignment** with the Group's Philosophical Concepts.

Because he is worthy of this confidence, the Team Member must be empowered by his Leader to **make things happen** in his business as soon as they have reached a mutual agreement through an Action Program.

2.1 ORGANIC GROWTH

A Large Organization with the Spirit of a Small Firm

Grooming the Next Generations

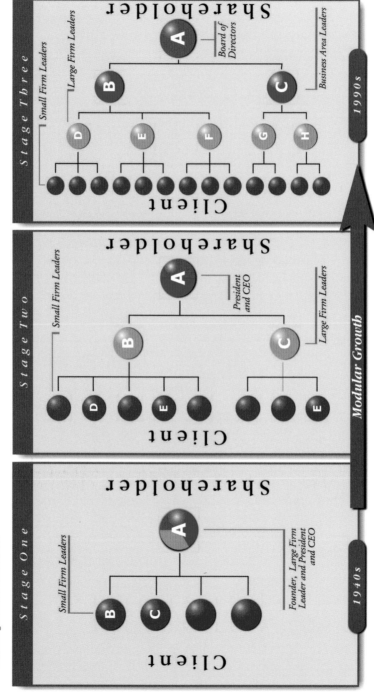

All members of the LINE that links the CLIENT and SHAREHOLDERS are simultaneously ENTREPRENEURS of their Businesses and each other's PARTNERS. They are therefore ENTREPRENEUR-PARTNERS working in different areas with varying responsibilities.
The maximum number of Entrepreneur-Partners COORDINATED and INTEGRATED by a single Leader is directly related to that Leader's abililiy and motivation as an EDUCATOR, because Leaders must share their TIME, PRESENCE, EXPERIENCE and EXAMPLE with their Team Members through continuous FOLLOW-UP, APPRAISAL AND JUDGMENT.

Modular Growth

Stage One — 1940s

Stage Two

Stage Three — 1990s

Thus conceived, planned delegation permits

- **permanent, direct** and **individual contact** with the Client, which is the basis for **survival;**

- **education through work,** with a view to grooming new and better Entrepreneurs and constantly improving everyone, which is the basis for **growth;** and

- the **integration** of mature Leaders, which is the basis for the Group's **perpetuity.**

Planned delegation is put into practice through the combined use of the following five tools of the **Communication System:**

Agendas;
Synopses;
Action Plan;
Action Program;
Reports, including Personal Narratives that shed light on the Report and resulting Synopsis, which can supplement the Action Program, followed by new Agendas and Synopses, thereby completing the constantly renewed entrepreneurial cycle of Follow-Up, Appraisal and Judgment.

2.1. *ACTION PLAN*

An Action Plan is a set of items comprising

- the **priorities** of the Large Firm's Leader; and

- the identification of the Small-Firm Leaders who can help transform these priorities into **results.**

The starting point for **defining** the Leader's **priorities** is the **opportunity to serve** a specific Client whose needs must be satisfied on the basis of the Group's **Philosophical Concepts,** Shareholders' **deliberations** and the **guidelines** provided by the Board of Directors, as well as the **expertise** of the Leader and his Team in their respective **Business.**

Through dialogue, negotiation and agreement, the Leader and his Team Member mutually influence one another until the Leader's **priorities** have been clearly defined, the Team Member has taken on and **assimilated** the priorities entrusted to him, and both are involved in and committed to **winning over** and **satisfying** the Client.

The Team Member's involvement and commitment are manifested in practice through the **Action Program** formulated by him to convert the Leader's **priority** into the **business** of serving and satisfying a specific Client.

2.2. Action Program

The Action Program through which the Team Member takes responsibility for the **priorities** entrusted to him by his Leader defines:

1. the Team Member's **business;**

2. the **philosophy** for managing that business;

3. the **results agreed upon** and corresponding **schedules;**

4. the **Team,** including people **Responsible** for **Results Centers** as well as those **Responsible** for providing the necessary **support;**

5. the **communication system** that will keep the Team Member simultaneously united with the Client and his Leader;

6. the business's **budget;**

7. how the **results** which the Team Member and his own Team have earned will be **shared;**

8. the **grooming of potential Substitutes** who must be prepared in advance in a suitable educational climate so that the Team Member can take on even greater challenges.

An Action Program is nothing more than a **proposal** for **serving** a given Client, together with the **commitment** to producing **results,** sharing them and **grooming potential Substitutes.**

Once he has received, negotiated and agreed upon his Team Members' Action Programs, the Leader must integrate them to obtain his own Action Program which, in turn, must be amended and/or endorsed by the Business Area Leader along the **Client → Shareholder** line.

2.3. *FOLLOW-UP, APPRAISAL AND JUDGMENT*

While the Team Member is carrying out his Action Program, he and his Leader communicate with each other constantly through the spoken word, supplemented by the written word and the language of numbers.

This will enable both of them jointly to follow up on the execution of the Team Member's Action Program and thereby appraise and judge the performance of both on the basis of hard facts.

Like follow-up, appraisal must be systematic, periodic and even daily, depending on the situation, circumstances and specific case.

As for the Large Firm's Leader, he must take into consideration:

1. the Small-Firm Leader's relationship with the Client;

2. the relationship between the Team in question and the Client's Team;

3. the execution of the work schedule in harmony with the financial schedule;

4. the evaluation and measurement of risks;

5. the identification of opportunities, including variables that could help improve the results and schedules previously agreed upon;

6. control over costs; and

7. his contribution to identifying **new** and **better Entrepreneurs** and educating them through work.

In his turn, the Team Member will appraise the effectiveness of his Leader's support.

Working from the basis of this reciprocal appraisal, which is constantly amended and/or endorsed, the Leader and his Team Member can individually judge whether they should continue working together or go their separate ways.

A distinction must be made between **appraisal** and **judgment.**

Appraisal is carried out jointly by the Leader and Team Member with the aim of improving their **performance** and **progress.**

Judgment, however, is an individual action whose ultimate purpose is to decide whether the Leader and Team Member should take their relationship further, as well as considering the prospects for the Team Member's **self-development.**

The basic tool for effecting follow-up, appraisal and judgment is the **periodic narrative** (verbal report).

This **periodic narrative** must be preceded by a **written report,** which is an **agenda** containing the figures required to understand the situation at any given moment, an accurate appraisal of the **intangible** and **tangible results** effectively achieved and their comparison with those agreed upon.

The Leader must familiarize himself with the report beforehand in order to be better prepared to **listen to** the Team Member's **narrative.**

Because the Leader is constantly providing Support to his Team Member, there are no "set dates" for dialogue between them.

The need for dialogue must always be determined by the emergence of **significant events** and **circumstances** that require the Leader's support.

At any time of day or night, even on weekends and holidays, the Leader must be available to listen to, advise and help his Team Member reach decisions.

By opening up his professional and personal life to his Team Member, the Leader is performing the role of an **Educator** while creating the basis for building up a true **friendship** between them.

When united by mutual **trust,** which generates **discipline, respect** and **friendship,** both will be able to better practice their **loyalty** to the Group as they tirelessly study ways to **improve** the Team Member's business.

Thanks to the **reciprocal trust** between the Leader and Team Member, their relationship will never be that of "**creditor vs. debtor,**" as both share the aim of **self-development.**

Constant study based on facts produced by follow-up, appraisal and judgment of **reciprocal performance** will enable them to continuously increase the **intellectual** and **operational productivity** of the **Small Firm,** and therefore those of the **Large Firm.**

3.   ENTREPRENEURIAL TASK

The Entrepreneurial Task is an ongoing process focused on

- **identifying, creating** and **winning over** a Client; and

- **satisfying** that Client.

The aim of the Entrepreneurial Task is to produce services and goods that, when measured, sold, billed and paid for, can be converted into **wealth** for the Client, the People who serve them, and Shareholders.

The Entrepreneurial Task consists of **two complementary parts:**

- the **first** is dedicated to winning over the Client and Partners who can help satisfy that Client; the emphasis lies on identifying **what is right** and creating the **moral wealth** that can lead to a proposal or tender and a contract; and

- the **second** focuses on **execution,** when the Client is satisfied by the Small Firm's Leader with the help of his respective Leader. The emphasis here is on **doing the right thing well** through the coordination and integration of results that will lead to the creation of **material wealth** while generating even more **moral wealth** in order to establish an **enduring relationship** with the Client.

These two parts are inseparable, because:

- **the person who wins over the Client must be responsible for their satisfaction;** and

- **the person who sells the service or product must deliver it to the Client.**

Every Line Member participates in the Entrepreneurial Task, whether they are the Leader of the Small Firm and Team who are in direct touch with the Client, or those who directly or indirectly provide **support,** including everyone from the Large Firm's Leader to the person Responsible for the Business Area in question.

> *The true Entrepreneur nurtures the entrepreneurial idea from its emergence to the transformation of what was produced into net results that are available in cash.*

This is the key to **successful decentralization** and **planned delegation,** thanks to the practice of **responsible freedom.**

As illustrated in figure 2.2, this is how the Entrepreneur exercises the **responsible freedom to**

- **realize the dream;**

2.2. MAKING DREAMS COME TRUE

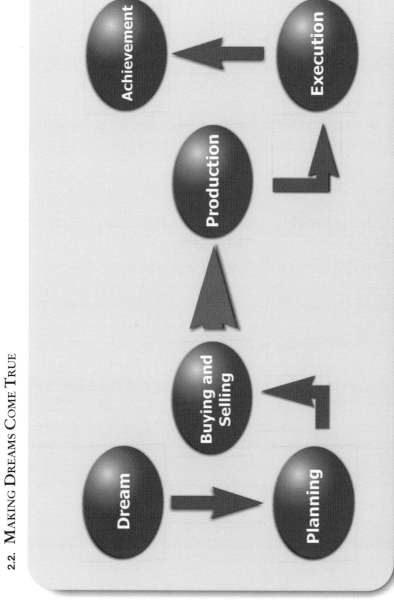

- **execute what was planned;** and

- **produce results as promised.**

If the **first** and **second parts** of the Entrepreneurial Task become **inseparable** within the **Small Firm,** then:

- the **commitment** to the Client's needs will **encourage** and **discipline** the realization of the dream;

- the "mortality rate" for **creative ideas** will be reduced; and

- the door to **"wasted time, energy and money"** will be closed, because planning divorced from reality places "a great deal of efficiency at the service of nonexistent effectiveness."

To err is human, and the incidence of errors increases between the dream and its fulfillment. Rather than tolerating errors, however, the Entrepreneur must identify and correct them promptly, even transforming them into opportunities to create, innovate and educate through work.

3.1. *OPPORTUNITY TO SERVE*

The process of winning over a Client starts with the adequate identification of the potential Client's needs and the transformation of those needs into the Leader's **priorities.**

When viewed in light of the needs of clearly visualized Clients, these priorities govern the **creative ideas** of the Leader and his Team Members.

Creative ideas become reality when the Leader and Team Member have identified what is valuable for the Client and therefore decisive when planning.

Once the Client's real needs have been identified, the creative ideas produced from the basis of the Client's needs can be transformed into **opportunities to serve.**

A key warning is in order here: the **opportunity to serve** presupposes that the Leader has **previously identified** a Team Member who is **available** and is best suited to creating a satisfied Client.

The **identification** and **availability** of the Small Firm's Leader is an **essential prerequisite** for characterizing an opportunity to serve.

And this Entrepreneur will be responsible for **winning over** the Client through whom the opportunity to serve will become a **business.**

3.2. *BUSINESS*

The term "business" is extremely ancient.

In its original simplicity, it was used to designate a bilateral relationship that arose as often as there were Clients for a given Businessperson.

Although the word business is both singular and plural, for a Businessperson **each Client represented a separate business.**

As a result of mass production, however, the bilateral relationship between Client and Businessperson has lost some of its original simplicity and purity.

At the same time, the term Business has come to designate an area or specific field of operations for diversified Companies.

Given the **option to decentralize** which the Odebrecht Group has taken since its beginnings, the "modern" and "abstract" meaning of the word Business should be used with caution.

The Odebrecht Group's Entrepreneurs should behave like Businesspersons, each of whom is engaged in business transacted with clearly individualized Clients regarding specific goods and services.

In order to answer the question **"what is my business?"** the Entrepreneur must continuously ask himself:

- Who is my Client?

- What are my entrepreneurial aims in regard to this Client?

- What goods and services must be supplied to create a satisfied Client?

- How can we make these goods and services better than ever?

- How should results, schedules and costs be negotiated?

Because his task is to keep each of his Clients satisfied and create enduring relationships with them, the Entrepreneur must:

- individualize each Client so that they **stand out** from the rest;

- identify what this individualized Client might consider valuable;

- clearly define his business with this Client; and

- make advance preparations to satisfy this specific Client.

The transformation of the opportunity to serve into a business can only take place at the moment when, having signed a contract or accepted a production order, the Small Firm's Leader:

- amends and/or endorses the Results Centers;

- puts together his Support Team;

- creates and establishes his Communication System; and

■ energizes the structure thus created through a continuous cycle of decisions and actions.

3.3. FIRST PART OF THE ENTREPRENEURIAL TASK

During the first part of this task, the Client is won over. The starting point is the **Philosophical Concepts, entrepreneurial aims** and **guidelines** provided by the Odebrecht Group's Shareholders.

By making these concepts, aims and guidelines his own, the Leader seeks to formulate a strategy through which the Group's **Moral** and **Material Assets** can be placed at his Client's service **in practice**.

This strategy arises from the adequate perception of the **overall situation** and the **situation desired** by all, detailed in an **Action Plan** that integrates **existing businesses** and establishes the direction for **creating** and **integrating new businesses** into the Large Firm.

When he is creative and furnished with a good Action Plan, the Leader can produce feasible ideas on the basis of the facts he comes to perceive. Thanks to systematic discipline, the Leader converts the **Client's needs** into **creative ideas,** and these into **priorities for service**.

Working from the basis of the priorities entrusted to him by his Leader, the Team Member studies the answers to the following questions for each specific Client:

– What does the Client want?

– What is valuable and makes the difference for this Client?

– Is this what they really need?

– How can I help them obtain the resources they require?

– When do they want them?

– Whom should I work with?

– What resources should I utilize?

– What results should I obtain?

– How should these results be shared?

Finding the **right answers** requires the **right amount of time,** and a great deal of coming-and-going will be necessary before an agreement emerges among the people who will be Responsible for Results Centers, the future Small-Firm Leader, and the Large Firm's Leader, regarding the best way of winning over and satisfying the Client.

At every stage of these comings-and-goings, each person's role will become increasingly clear to everyone concerned, and closer to **what is right.**

Having built up this agreement, the Proposal or Tender to be presented to the Client can be formulated by clearly defining the business, which means determining:

- **what** to produce;

- **how** to produce it;

- **when;**

- **with whom;**

- **for how much;** and

- **how** to transform invoices into **net results** available in Cash.

Once the Client has approved the proposal, the essence of the Action Program for the Small- Firm Leader responsible for the future venture will also have been formulated.

It should be stressed that this Leader's Action Program is nothing more than the Proposal or Tender submitted to the Client, to which the following have been added:

- the basis for Sharing the Results and

- the Small-Firm Leader's responsibilities regarding **education through work** with a view to improving himself and grooming **new** and **better Entrepreneurs.**

3.4. *Second Part* of *the Entrepreneurial Task*

To continue examining the Entrepreneurial Task under the lens of the Small Firm's operations, once his Action Program has been agreed upon with his Leader, the Team Member must amend and/or endorse:

- his Results Centers, working with the person Responsible for each of them;

- his lean, flexible Support Team, which must be adapted to the Client's specific needs in terms of time and geography; and

- his Communication System.

From this point forward, the Leader must act like a Team Member of the individual he leads, joining in the quest for shared success.

During the **first part** of the Entrepreneurial Task, **the right thing** is identified.

During the **second part,** the challenge consists of doing **the right thing** better than ever.

In view of their commitment to **productivity,** in addition to executing their plans, the Team must **surpass** the **expected results in practice.**

The true Entrepreneur is distinguished by his dissatisfaction with the results agreed upon.

This dissatisfaction enables him to **exceed** the Client's **highest expectations** and therefore those of the Shareholders regarding the Small Firm's Leader and his Large Firm's Leader.

To the extent that each person Responsible for a Results Center achieves and surpasses what has been agreed upon, the Small Firm's Leader

- integrates the results achieved;

- transforms them into the goods and services the Client wants;

- receives payment of invoices;

- pays his debts;

- shares the results; and

- produces net results in Cash, which are available to the Leader.

3.5. *INVOLVEMENT, COMMITMENT AND ENTHUSIASM*

Ensuring the Client's satisfaction is a process that requires the **contributions** of **each** and **every** Partner.

The Client, the Small Firm's Leader, his Team and the Large Firm's Leader, as well as Suppliers, Community Representatives and Government Officials, among others, must have a sense of unity within the same **climate of cooperation.**

The Small Firm's Leader plays a decisive role in creating this climate because his greatest challenge consists of obtaining the **involvement, commitment** and **enthusiasm** of those who can directly or indirectly influence the course of events.

If each and every Partner is involved, committed and enthusiastic about the same **cause,** the natural consequence will be the **success** of their **common enterprise.**

This is what could be termed **total commitment,** which directs everyone's **strengths** in the search for identical aims.

4. RESULTS

The continuous appreciation of Shareholders' **Moral** and **Material Assets** enables more and better results to **flow** from the **Client** towards the **Shareholder.**

These **results** can be either **intangible** or **tangible; short-** or **long-term.**

What is essential is that they contribute to the Odebrecht Group's **Survival, Growth** and **Perpetuity.**

4.1. *SURVIVAL*

A Company's survival depends on its **productivity** and consequent **profitability**, as well as **image** and **liquidity**.

The priority conferred on each of these results will vary according to the **time** and **circumstances**.

The starting point for building up these results is **discipline**, which must be instilled from the basis of the Small Firm's Results Centers.

It is important to distinguish **survival** from **"subsistence."**

"Subsistence" means equalizing results and expenses.

Survival means generating net results that are available in Cash in a sufficient quantity to finance growth.

4.2. *GROWTH*

When **healthy**, growth is **organic** and **balanced**. Growth is very different from **"swelling,"** which leads to **"deterioration"** and **"ruin."**

The **essential prerequisite** for growth is the availability of a **Small-Firm Leader** who is prepared, motivated and challenged to lead the effort to win over and satisfy each of the Clients he has been chosen to serve.

The Small Firm's Leader, it should be added, must be linked through a relationship of **mutual trust** with the people Responsible for Results Centers who make up his Team, and his own Leader, because such confidence is **indispensable** for producing **discipline, respect** and **friendship** among them, as well as their **loyalty** to the Group.

Once this essential prerequisite has been met, **healthy growth** will also depend upon:

- **innovation**;

- **education through work**, which helps groom **new** and **better Entrepreneurs**;

- **technological advances**; and

- the formation of **Intangible** and **Tangible Assets**.

4.3. *PERPETUITY*

Perpetuity is a **dream.**

A dream for those who derive a sense of satisfaction from helping groom successive generations of **new** and **better Entrepreneurs.**

Entrepreneurs who, once transformed into Leaders, can share the same dream by helping develop and integrate new **Entrepreneurs** who are **better still.**

To attain Perpetuity, the Group's Leaders must be permanently dedicated to

- **grooming** and **integrating new** and **better generations** of **Entrepreneurs** and **Teams;**

- obtaining increasing **returns** on Shareholders' **investments;** and

- promoting the safety of People and Assets, thereby fulfilling the organization's **social responsibility.**

There is just one prerequisite for making their dedication successful:

> *loyalty to the Group, expressed through the application of the philosophical concepts, entrepreneurial aims and deliberations of the Shareholders.*

5.   THE COMPANY'S SOCIAL RESPONSIBILITY

At the Odebrecht Group, the **Company's social responsibility** means the **Entrepreneur's social responsibility.**

Odebrecht Group Entrepreneurs fulfill their social responsibility by:

- satisfying their Clients with services and goods that improve the quality of life of the Communities in which they are present;

- contributing to the social, economic, technological and entrepreneurial development of those Communities;

- creating work and development opportunities for People through means including the reinvestment of the results achieved;

- generating wealth for the Government and Communities by paying taxes and tariffs and compensating Suppliers, Members and Shareholders; and

- always caring responsibly for the Environment in all of their business ventures.

In order for this to take place on a permanent basis, these Entrepreneurs must obtain **productivity, liquidity, image** and the resulting **profitability.** This means attaining the essential prerequisites for their Company's **survival.**

Only a Company that enjoys such productivity, liquidity and a good image can fulfill its commitments on time and maintain a good relationship with the community.

Once its **survival** has been guaranteed, the Company's **organic, healthy growth** must be ensured.

And by maintaining this **organic, healthy growth,** the Company can forge ahead on the path towards **perpetuity.**

This is why, within the Odebrecht Group, **survival, growth** and **perpetuity** are synonymous with the Company's social **responsibility** and therefore the watchwords which its Members must put into practice in order to achieve fulfillment as **model Citizens** of the Communities to which they belong.

By **surviving, growing** and **perpetuating itself,** the Group can make **additional** and **permanent contributions** to the Communities in which it is present, such as the educational projects supported by the Odebrecht Foundation, and the Companies' sponsorship of research and projects that contribute to the production of the finest expressions of the arts and culture, as well as promoting cultural exchange between nations.

Standards for Applying the Odebrecht Entrepreneurial Technology

The Odebrecht Group has a **Hallmark** that sums up its **Entrepreneurial Technology:**

a Large Firm with the spirit of a Small Firm.

Continuously applying and adding value to this Hallmark requires **competence**.

Competence is a virtue that the potential Entrepreneur must acquire while exercising his **spirit** through **hard, creative** and **disciplined work,** which generates **wealth,** while constantly seeking to improve **productivity** and the resulting **profitability,** as well as the **liquidity** and good **image** of the business under his leadership.

The drive to achieve the following aims was a constant factor in the life of my Father, Emílio Odebrecht:

- identifying and recruiting People with **spirit** and the **potential** to learn, whether they were mature Human Beings with expertise in conventional methods, or promising Youths. All of them had to be capable of developing themselves and contributing to the growth of Emílio Odebrecht & Cia., the construction firm mentioned in the Preface;

- creating a climate that promoted the self-development of these People through day-to-day practice at the construction site;

- putting together synergetic and contributive Teams made up of Supervisors, Foremen, Artisans and Laborers; and

- continuously following up on, appraising and judging these Teams and People with the aim of **selecting** and **keeping on** the **best.**

Such teams, led by experienced Supervisors, were the starting point for building up Construtora Norberto Odebrecht.

Thanks to the Supervisors trained by Emílio Odebrecht, the newborn Group was able to groom new, effective and contributive Teams and thereby multiply its ability to be present and produce **results** simultaneously in a large number of small projects.

These effective, contributive teams, it should be recalled, were made up of People who were constantly **appraised** and **judged** – when possible, on a **daily** basis.

To continue growing and making constant technological advances, the Group started bringing in Young People recruited from Universities.

Its sites became campuses that groomed Entrepreneurs who are now in their Second or even Third Ages.

For Odebrecht, **education through work** has always been and should continue to be synonymous with harmonizing the Individual's **development** and the organization's **growth.**

With higher and higher levels of performance, we must institutionalize the Group's role as a **magnetic pole** that attracts Young People who want to become Entrepreneurs.

This confers even more **priority** on the task which the Group's Leaders cannot and must not delegate: constantly **educating** good new Entrepreneurs **through work.**

In light of their educational responsibilities, each Entrepreneur within the Group must be

■ an extraordinary Talent Scout;

■ an exemplary Educator; and

■ a Leader who is prepared to follow up on, appraise and judge the performance of his Team Members with a view to selecting and integrating the finest.

To best perform his educational role, each Leader must adapt or if necessary change his **attitudes** and **behaviors** towards Human Beings with a view to concentrating on the appraisal and judgment of his Team Members' **entrepreneurial spirit** and **potential for development.**

With the aim of encouraging suitable attitudes and behaviors, the following chapters present the **standards** which should influence the way the Group's Members **think** and **act.**

What is a **standard**?

According to the dictionaries, this term means:

■ something that is established as a model for comparison, judgment or measurement;

- a principle used to distinguish right from wrong;

- discernment, circumspection and prudence;

- a means of judging things and/or People.

In the Entrepreneur's case, a **standard** is all these things, with a focus on:

- increasing and consolidating his **philosophical grounding;**

- guiding his **day-to-day actions;**

- helping produce **Results;** and

- adding value to the **Moral** and **Material Assets** directly or indirectly entrusted to him by the Shareholders.

Having understood the meaning of the word, we can now engage in a detailed analysis of the **General Standards** established to guide the practice of **educating** the Odebrecht Group's Entrepreneurs **through work.**

Eight **General Standards** must guide the attitudes and behaviors of Odebrecht Group Entrepreneurs.

1. *The Individual is the measure of all the Group's values.*

Productivity is the key to ensuring the Client's **satisfaction today**, **tomorrow** and **always,** because it is

- synonymous with **more quality** in **less time,** at a **lower cost;** and

- the source of **profitability**, which finances growth and remunerates Shareholders.

Because the Odebrecht Group is made up of Human Beings, it follows that the organization will only be **productive** if it is comprised of **productive** Human Beings.

Since the starting point is the Individual, the Odebrecht Group must constantly identify and select Human Beings with spirit, character, talent, motivation and aptitude, as well as keeping on and integrating those who prove to be the **best** in terms of **productivity.**

This is the only means of ensuring that Odebrecht has **Future Leaders** capable of adopting **attitudes** and **behaviors** suited to the organization's growth requirements.

2. *The Entrepreneur must have a complete mastery of his business in order to satisfy the Client and Shareholder simultaneously.*

The Entrepreneur has gained a **mastery** of his **business** when he

■ has identified the right Client;

■ knows what they want and need to be satisfied;

■ can define the proposal or tender, schedule and price that will be billed to the Client;

■ has satisfied the Client while generating productivity, profitability, liquidity and a good image; and

■ has contributed to his own development and that of his Team Members by means of education through work, thereby grooming everyone to give even better service in the Future.

To achieve all of this, the Entrepreneur must have an in-depth knowledge of his business and effectively apply that knowledge; but he must also be involved and emotionally committed to his work in order to interact and share common aims with his Client.

Only People who enjoy what they do and are fulfilled by their work have the intellectual curiosity to study new things, seek more productive ways of bringing them about and, above all, initiate Young People into the mysteries of the business and motivate them to love what they do.

3. *Education through work is an integral part of the Entrepreneurial Task.*

The **First Part** of the **Entrepreneurial Task** delineates the **dream of serving** a given Client through the **planning** which generates **moral wealth** and **trust** between the Client, the Entrepreneur and the Partners, and consequently **wins** this Client **over.**

During the **Second Part** of the **Entrepreneurial Task,** these plans are **executed** with a view to generating **material wealth** and consolidating **moral wealth** with the aim of **satisfying** the Client and establishing a **lasting relationship** with them.

Each part of the Entrepreneurial Task depends on the other; they are complementary.

Similarly, **identifying, winning over** and **satisfying** the Client is inseparable from the task of **educating** Odebrecht Group Entrepreneurs **through work.**

4. *Those who provide services to the people Responsible for results must always be oriented toward opportunities and results.*

Within the Group, support can only be offered to those who want, need and can use such help to identify opportunities and obtain or improve results.

Otherwise, it is a waste of time, energy and money; it is harmful and creates dependency between those who request and those who offer any kind of help.

5. ***The Individual has the right to a share of the results he has directly helped produce and which can be measured, billed and paid for by the Client.***

The people who perform their entrepreneurial task as Line Members are willing to take risks to satisfy their Client while achieving and surpassing the results agreed upon with their immediate Leader.

Each Entrepreneur in the Group must establish a relationship based on **partnership** with his immediate Leader, which must be grounded on a very simple rule:

> ***the People who stand to gain the most are those who produce the best results.***

Being solely in command of the sharing of results, which is determined according to specific standards established in his Action Program, the Entrepreneur must previously determine (through mutual agreement with his Team Members) the shares each will receive in the amount to which he is entitled.

The manner in which the Entrepreneur appraises and judges his Team Members reflects his own **character** and therefore gives his immediate Leader an **objective standard** with which to judge him.

6. *The Entrepreneur must always be open to recognizing and quickly rectifying his errors.*

To err is human.

If this is true, then those who work the most will err the most when seeking further achievements and accomplishments.

That is why the Individual can only be **successful** when, during his day-to-day labors, he is open to quickly **identifying** his errors and **rectifying** them faster still.

According to an ancient fable, the Individual finds it easier to identify other people's errors than his own.

Those imbued with **spirit** and the **commitment to success** will only be interested in identifying **what is right,** rather than determining "who is right" and "who is wrong."

This means they must be open to receiving **frank, constructive** and **honest** criticism from people who work with them and are equally committed to everyone's **success.**

The virtue of recognizing one's own errors ennobles the Individual.

For this reason, those who are unconditionally willing to analyze and rectify the errors shown them by their Co-Workers are even nobler.

7. *The image that matters and makes the difference is built up in the Community from the basis of each individual Client's satisfaction, and our commitment to the Community's well-being.*

As a service provider working with individualized Clients, it is the duty of each Entrepreneur-Partner to build up an **image** based on **competence**, **transparency** and **probity** in the eyes of their Client, as well as Suppliers, other Partners and the general Community.

Although this is the **basis** for the **image** held of the Group by Public Opinion, another equally indispensable pillar is each Odebrecht Entrepreneur's fulfillment of his civic duty as a Citizen committed to the well-being of his Community.

8. *Group Members are responsible for promoting their own health and that of each of their Team Members, as well as occupational safety, quality of life and environmental conservation in the Communities in which they work.*

From the Communities in which it is present, the Group receives healthy Human Beings who are prepared to do productive work and generate wealth.

When integrating itself into a Community, the Group begins working in accordance with that Community's standards of **occupational safety**, **quality of life** and **environmental conservation**.

The organization must repay these Communities by **promoting individual health**, **safety** in all its operations, **quality of life** and **environmental conservation** with an emphasis on **prevention.**

In the specific case of its Members' personal hygiene, no matter how intensive the Group's efforts may be, it must always be clearly understood that

> *responsibility for health promotion starts with the Individual,*

whose Leader is responsible for **heightening** his **awareness** and **motivating** him in this regard.

In conclusion, the Odebrecht Group's overall responsibility in all the areas mentioned here must be put into practice through effective measures taken by each Small Firm's Leader together with his Team. It must also be the subject of ongoing dialogue during all stages of the cycle of negotiating and executing each Individual's Action Program.

Having covered these eight **General Standards,** I can now go on to discuss **Specific Standards.** These are **operational,** and should serve as a guide for the day-to-day work of everyone in the Odebrecht Group.

Standards for
Applying the
Odebrecht
Entrepreneurial
Technology

CHAPTER 4

*Operating
Standards*

The **operating standards** which should guide the work of the Odebrecht Group's Members are grouped here under specific topics, classified according to the General Standards from which they extend, to wit:

The Individual and his Performance;
Mastery of the Business;
Education through Work;
Providing Support;
Partnership and Sharing Results;
Overcoming Errors;
the Group's Image; and
Health, Safety, Quality of Life and the Environment.

Rather than being a "straight-jacket," this classification should be considered merely as a contribution to the **intellectual organization** and **disciplined actions** of the organization's Members, which are fundamental.

1. THE INDIVIDUAL AND PERFORMANCE

1st STANDARD

The Group's **Aim** – the pursuit of **Survival, Growth** and **Perpetuity** – is the **beacon** that guides its Leaders and Team Members on the path of **ethics** and **morality** and therefore towards the realization of their **ideals** and **objectives.**

2nd STANDARD

The Group's Leaders must identify the **Demanding Client** who is constantly questioning while seeking the **best quality,** the **shortest deadlines** and the **lowest costs.**

This is the Client that interests them and must be won over so that the Group's Entrepreneurs can best develop themselves.

3rd STANDARD

All **decisions** pertaining to Human Beings are **strategic,** because it is through them that the Leader can achieve his **priorities.**

The **most** strategic decisions have to do with the **development** of Line Members directly committed to their Client's satisfaction.

4th STANDARD

The **effectiveness** of their joint efforts presupposes **free, qualified** and **extensive communication** between Human Beings so that they can share in the fulfillment of these **priorities** and a commitment to them.

5th STANDARD

The Leader must build up this **communication** and help his Team Members obtain **information** as well as accustoming them to **measuring** this information and **expressing** it **numerically** so that he can follow up on, appraise and judge his Team Members' self-development.

Through **communication** and **information,** the Leader and Team Member deepen and consolidate their **confidence in each other.**

6th STANDARD

To obtain adequate information, in addition to **measuring** and **expressing it numerically,** the Entrepreneur must have a **mastery** of his Business. This means **understanding** it, **reflecting** on its individual characteristics and having the **competence** to take **rapid** decisions and action.

Discipline produces **respect,** which consolidates **trust** between the Leader and Team Member, who are permanently interrelated by **effective communication** and the exchange of **efficient information.**

7th STANDARD

One indicator of the **commitment** of each person Responsible for Results to educating new and better Entrepreneurs is the frequency with which he deals with this subject in meetings held with his immediate **Leader** and **Team Members.**

The agendas and minutes of the true Leader must always contain a **special section** devoted to this subject.

8th STANDARD

To be admitted into the Group, an Individual must possess:

- **character;**

- **potential** for self-development;

- the **motivation** to give **service humbly,** rather than wanting to "be served";

- the **desire** and **motivation** to learn;

- **aptitude** for working in the specific area to which he might be assigned; and

- **tenacity, persistence** and other virtues that effectively characterize him as an Individual with real potential for self-development.

9th STANDARD

For those who are just beginning their career at Odebrecht, the best entryway is the **Small Firm,** where real production takes place and the Client is effectively served. This is where what is **right** and **wrong** takes place.

10th STANDARD

The **Knowledgeable Individual** should preferably be admitted as a youth, through an **internship.** When he is an adult, however, he must be hired after a **trial period** that will give him and his immediate Leader time to decide whether it is in both their interests to establish a lasting relationship. This is the "engagement" that should precede the Individual's "marriage" to the organization.

11th STANDARD

During the period immediately following the newcomer's arrival, when he begins associating with his Co-Workers, his immediate Leader must determine whether that Team Member not only has **character** but is an Individual endowed with the other necessary virtues.

If the newcomer has these merits, then:

■ he will prove to be **humble** and **unassuming,** impervious to the "temptations of power" and devoid of "vanity"; and

■ free of the weakness of "arrogance," which is inherent to whose who want "to be served."

12th STANDARD

Once the trial period has ended and the newcomer has demonstrated that he does indeed possess the necessary virtues, his immediate Leader must follow up on, appraise and judge him with the aim of discovering whether this Team Member is capable of

- identifying the **current status** of his business as well as the **future status** desired;

- subordinating the **present** to the **future;**

- visualizing **Survival** as the pre-requisite for **Growth** and this Growth as the pre-requisite for **Perpetuity;** and

- bringing about, in **practice, a dynamic balance** between everything he has visualized.

13th STANDARD

Another inseparable part of the follow-up, appraisal and judgment of the newly hired Individual is the analysis of his capacity to make use of the **Five Rules** for achieving **Effectiveness,** which are:

- **saving time,** which presupposes planning;

- **focusing** on **contribution,** which involves frankness,
  teamwork,

self-development,
overall development, and
synergy;

- making the **strengths** of the **People** he leads and the **force of circumstance productive;**

- **concentrating** on the **priorities** that make the difference, which requires more **courage** than **analysis;** and

- without neglecting **method,** giving precedence to **decisions** that make the greatest **impact** on the **results.**

14th STANDARD

Job rotation is **acceptable** as a **stimulus** so that the Knowledgeable Individual who is a Line or Support Team Member can better familiarize himself with the Group. However, it should be used sparingly and always be tied to the aim of **grooming** him through repeated exposure to **increasing challenges** and the unfailing **support** of his Leader.

2.   MASTERY OF THE BUSINESS

15th STANDARD

All other results depend on **productivity,** which is achieved when the Individual Responsible for Results **knows** what he is doing and how to improve it:

- when continuously creating and innovating with the aim of obtaining **ever-increasing quality** in **less time** and at a **lower cost;**

- when combating "waste" in all of its forms by conserving his Team Members' **energies** as well as natural and material resources;

- when creating opportunities and situations that encourage his own **self-development** and that of his Team Members; and therefore,

- when making more and better **liquid results** flow into the Group's treasury.

16th STANDARD

Productivity, like **profitability, image** and the resulting **liquidity,** must be ensured from the beginning of the Entrepreneurial Task and maintained throughout the **two parts** of this task (**winning over** and **satisfying** the **Client**) through permanent **follow-up, appraisal** and **judgment.**

Among other important points, the **Business,** its **Philosophy** and **Results** are established in the **Action Program,** together with **Schedules, Organization** and **Costs.**

Therefore, this is a basic tool that must be used to guide the search for productivity in the Team Member's business.

17th STANDARD

When, in the course of the **Entrepreneurial Task,** the Action Plan and Program are formulated and amended and/or endorsed when appropriate, the search for productivity will become a constant factor in the Leader's and Team Member's relationship.

18th STANDARD

The Large and Small Firms must be kept **lean, agile** and **flexible.** To do so, they require constant exercise to avoid a build-up of "flab."

19th STANDARD

In order to keep their focus in the battle against "waste," the Leader and Team Member must ask themselves:

"Are the Client and Shareholders willing to cover the cost of this service?"

If the answer is "no," the service must be eliminated.

20th STANDARD

The struggle against "waste" must involve everyone in the Odebrecht Group.

The people Responsible for Support must particularly ask themselves these questions on a permanent basis:

"What is useless or outdated about our work and should be discarded?"

"What can we do better to make our job more effective and less of a burden on the Group?"

"What should we start doing?"

21st STANDARD

In the struggle against "waste," the Leader must always encourage each Team Member to **simplify** his work and **streamline services, schedules** and **costs** while ensuring **quality,** the **Client's satisfaction** and the **safety** of his own Team Members.

22nd STANDARD

The Team Member must learn that the quest for higher **quality** and **streamlined schedules** and **costs** is not circumstantial or episodic. It is a permanent effort.

He must also involve his Team in this task and thereby demonstrate in practice that **productivity** is the key to making their work sounder while obtaining greater rewards.

23rd STANDARD

The Leader must warn his Team Members to avoid one of the most pernicious forms of waste, which is the growth of **fixed costs** as a percentage of total expenses.

Before creating **new Results Centers** and **Support Teams** and **hiring personnel** to provide the services the Client wants and is willing to pay for, the Team Member must ask himself:

"Can we team up with a partner to provide these services and garner savings for the Client and the Group?"

24th STANDARD

The Large-Firm and Small-Firm Leaders must always ask themselves:

"Is the cost of each of my Results Centers and Support compatible with the results they are producing?"

If the answer is "no," the Results Center or Support must be eliminated or replaced by teaming up with a **partner** when it is indispensable.

25th STANDARD

In addition to being attuned to the specific dynamics of the Large Firm, the **Knowledgeable People** who comprise it must be **as close as possible to the Small Firm** in order to sense the **Client's needs** and identify possible "sources of waste."

Any waste of time, energy or money marks the beginning of human ruin and degradation.

3. EDUCATION THROUGH WORK

26th STANDARD

The **aim** of **education through work** is to promote the Individual's **overall development.**

27th STANDARD

Each Individual's performance as an **Educator** and **Learner** can only be appraised to the extent that he helps groom **new** and **better** Entrepreneurs and prepares to take on increasing challenges.

28th STANDARD

Each Small Firm's Leader has a **responsibility** that **cannot be delegated:** creating favorable conditions for the self-development of his Team Members and integrating the results within his sphere of operations.

29th STANDARD

The effective **grooming** and **integration** of **new** and **better Entrepreneurs** heading healthy, agile and lean Small Firms that effectively contribute to the production of **resources available for investment** is the only suitable standard for appraising the Individual Responsible for the Large Firm's work as an **Educator.**

30th STANDARD

The Individual Responsible for the Large Firm is especially charged with establishing **where** and **how** to identify and recruit Knowledgeable People, given the individual characteristics of the Small Firms under his leadership and the Odebrecht Group's **Path.**

31st STANDARD

Particularly by sharing his **time, presence, experience** and **example**, the Leader must **follow up on, appraise** and **judge** each Team Member with the aim of helping him achieve professional, financial and psychological fulfillment as a Member of the Odebrecht Group, and give it his **loyalty.**

32nd STANDARD

The true Educator must possess personal relations skills and adopt attitudes and behaviors that serve as an example for his Team Members. Above all, however, what distinguishes him is the **spirit of service.** This means taking genuine pleasure in **giving of himself** on behalf of the self-development of the People under his responsibility.

33rd STANDARD

To be successful in his task as an **Educator,** the Large Firm's Leader must practice the **Pedagogy of Presence,** which means offering his **time, presence, experience** and **example** to each of his Team Members.

The Leader must especially adopt the following **attitudes** and **behaviors** in his relationship with his Team Member:

- **frankness,** on the basis of **what is right;**

- **receptivity** when challenged and confronted by the Team Member;

- **empathy,** putting himself in his Team Member's place and thereby perceiving his desires, difficulties and problems as though they were his own;

- **support,** to minimize the Team Member's **weaknesses** and maximize his **strengths;**

- **respect,** when accepting the Team Member as he is, even if he has qualities the Leader dislikes;

- **questioning,** practiced in the right manner at the right time to challenge and confront the Team Member;

- **discernment,** to perceive when the Team Member needs help; and

- **humility,** to learn from interactions with his Team Members.

34th STANDARD

To give even better service as an Educator, the Leader must also have interpersonal relations **skills** in order to make it clear that he is available and interested in talking with the Team Member.

Some of these skills include:

- **knowing how to ask questions,** encouraging the Team Member to make his **strengths,** those of the other **Human Beings** with whom he interacts and the **force of circumstance** more productive;

- **knowing how to give answers,** so that the Team Member can clearly understand the Leader's opinions and decisions;

- **knowing how to individualize,** when clearly defining the share of responsibility that falls to the Team Member and himself;

- **knowing how to provide support,** giving it in advance when necessary;

- **knowing how to acquire** and **transfer knowledge** as well as to **develop** his own **skills** and those of his Team Member; and

- **knowing how to make** his and his Team Member's **knowledge productive,** with a view to satisfying the Client and Shareholders.

35th STANDARD

The Learner must learn and even be **encouraged** to **think** before **answering,** as well as to **reflect** before taking **action,** because thoughtless answers and actions rarely lead to **good results.**

4. PROVIDING SUPPORT

36th STANDARD

All types of **support** are aimed at **overcoming weaknesses, multiplying strengths** and/or **saving** the **time** of those who receive it. There is nothing "shameful" about admitting one's **weaknesses** and seeking to overcome them. It demonstrates the Leader's **humility,** as well as his commitment to **surpassing** the **results** agreed upon.

37th STANDARD

Those who provide support take on the Action Program of the Individual who receives their support.

Therefore, the Leader's Action Program is the basis from which each Member of the Support Team must **plan** and **execute his tasks.**

Depending on the Client, circumstances and time, the Leader's need for support will change, along with the tasks of those who provide it.

This means that each Member of his Team must be sufficiently **flexible** and **agile** to constantly reformulate their tasks so that their **efficiency** is placed at the service of the Leader's **effectiveness.**

It should be observed that:

■ some tasks are routine and permanent while others are specific and transitory, which makes them unique; and

■ the Individual **Responsible for Support** must add to, supplement and maximize the **Leader's strengths.**

5. PARTNERSHIP AND RESULTS SHARING

38th STANDARD

The moment he has established a **partnership** with his Team Member, the Leader can

■ help the Team Member **clearly define** his **business** and its corresponding **philosophy;**

■ help him choose the unit of measurement he will use to **numerically express** the **results expected** from his business, as well as its **schedules** and **costs;**

- appraise the Team Member's **character** and other moral and intellectual virtues;

- measure the real contribution which this **Team Member** is making to the production of **resources available for reinvestment,** which will finance the **growth** of the Group Companies and contribute to the organization's **perpetuity;**

- negotiate the remuneration to which the Team Member will be entitled as a result of his effective contribution;

- help this Team Member realize his potential for self-development; and

- integrate him with the Group as a **good new Entrepreneur.**

39th STANDARD

Within the Odebrecht Group, each Partner builds up his own remuneration according to the contribution he makes to **improving** the results of his specific business.

Therefore, the results agreed upon and schedules for this specific business must be **measured** and **expressed numerically** so that they can be compared with the actual results.

It is through this constant comparison (conducted daily if possible) that the Partner educates himself, and the need to **measure** and **express** the results of his business numerically enters his DNA, together with the constant need to improve them.

40th STANDARD

In the case of the Small Firm, its Leader's **priority** is contributing to the Odebrecht Group's **Survival.**

The Small Firm's Leader makes this contribution when he obtains **productivity, profitability, liquidity** and **image,** and consequently **resources that are available in Cash and ready to be reinvested** by the Group.

These **resources,** which must be **available for reinvestment and have actually entered the Group's treasury,** should be the basis for calculating the Small-Firm Leader's **remuneration.**

41st STANDARD

The **priority** of the Individual Responsible for the Large Firm is to ensure its **growth** and thereby contribute to the **growth** of the Group by making **strategic** and **effective** decisions that promote

- **synergy** in his Team;

- **productivity** in the **Small Firms;** and

- the resulting **satisfaction** of the Clients of the Small Firms under his responsibility.

This Individual promotes the growth of his Large Firm to the extent that he integrates **new** and **better** Entrepreneurs who are capable of satisfying a growing number of Clients.

Therefore, the remuneration due to the Individual Responsible for the Large Firm must be based on the **quality** and **quantity** of the Entrepreneurs and Teams organized as Small Firms capable of producing **more and more available resources in the Group's treasury, ready for investment.**

42nd STANDARD

The contribution which each Support Team Member makes to his Leader's **success** involves so many **nuances** that only the Leader, through permanent interaction, will have enough **discernment** to **appraise** the Team Member's **performance** and negotiate suitable remuneration with that Individual.

43rd STANDARD

Support Team Members will receive a **portion** of the **share** to which their Leader is entitled, according to previously negotiated standards.

44th STANDARD

The **share** that an **officer** Responsible for Results offers his Team Members is an objective standard by which that officer's immediate Leader can **judge** him.

45th STANDARD

In an increasingly **interdependent** world, Partnership must be practiced both inside and outside the Group, because **cooperation with other companies** can prove decisive to achieving the aim of ensuring the Clients' satisfaction.

More than just **outsourcing,** the Odebrecht Group must engage in **partnering.**

Identifying and **winning over** a **new Partner** and entering into **new forms of partnership** represent unique learning opportunities to which the Leader and his Team must all be committed.

During this task, the starting point must be the identification of the Partner's **character** and true willingness to develop himself in harmony with the Odebrecht Group's growth.

46th STANDARD

It is the Large-Firm Leader's duty to prepare his Team Members to work productively and synergetically with other Companies that are motivated to enter into **partnerships** or other forms of cooperation.

6.   OVERCOMING ERRORS

47th STANDARD

The Team Member must be convinced that he has to apply the Group's **culture** in the right manner and with redoubled vigor, which means changing **attitudes** and **behaviors** that are no longer productive. While refraining from changing this culture or introducing "fads" and "imports" into the **common language** spoken in the Group Companies, he must also take care to question things when he deems that improvements can be made in this culture.

48th STANDARD

It is the Leader's duty to teach the Team Member that, before rushing off to "do different things," he must demonstrate his ability to solve **today's** problems in less time, at a lower cost and with the best **results.**

49th STANDARD

The Leader must be aware that the Team Member will only adopt the right attitudes and behaviors if he has been sufficiently encouraged and motivated.

The attitudes and behaviors that must be encouraged and motivated include those related to the practice of **effective partnership,** which presupposes **initiative, creativity, innovation** and **action** with a view to producing **more** and **better results.**

50th STANDARD

Ailments and accidents that affect the **leaves, branches** and **trunk** of a **tree** can be combated with medicine or, using more extreme methods, by lopping off the diseased portion.

Diseases that attack the **roots** are deadly, however, because they prevent the tree from absorbing **nutrients** and impede the **production** and **circulation** of **sap.**

In the Group Companies, **results** are the **sap,** the **Communication System** is the **conducting tissue,** and the **Small Firms** are the **roots.**

This is why the **health** of the **Small Firm,** which is linked to its Large Firm as **part** of a **federation,** must be the priority focus of attention for everyone in the Group.

51st STANDARD

When the Leader has adequately practiced the **Pedagogy of Presence** by sharing his **time, presence, experience** and **example** with his Team Members, "audits" and "supervision" will be unnecessary because, rather than focusing on "who is right" and "who is wrong," the Leader and each of his Team Members will focus on identifying **what is right** and doing it better than ever.

52nd STANDARD

Both the Large and Small Firms require a **Communication System** capable of aiming their operations towards **bull's eyes success.**

It should be recalled that, rather than being "cold" and "impersonal," the "tools" used in Communication must be warmed up by **frank, trustworthy** and **honest dialogue** between the Leader and Team Member, as well as **friendship** between them, shared **loyalty** to the Group and, in particular, their mutual **involvement** and **commitment** to adding value to the **Odebrecht Hallmark:**

*a **Large Firm** with the spirit of a **Small Firm.***

This Communication System is comprised of the following **tools:**

Action Plan;
Action Program;
Periodic reports and narratives; and
Agendas and Minutes,

which regulate **dialogue, negotiation** and **agreement** while generating **synergy** between the Leader and Team Member.

53rd STANDARD

The Leaders responsible for cooperation with other Companies must work with the Leaders of those Companies to constantly **follow up on, appraise** and **judge** the quality of the **communication** between the Partners and the **results** obtained through their joint efforts.

That is how confidence is built up between Partners and how Human Beings promote their self-development and contribute to the self-development of others.

54th STANDARD

Surpassing what was planned is both a consequence of and requirement for **success,** because it reinforces self-esteem and self-confidence while helping the Learner achieve the stage of self-help, self-management and self-responsibility. These are the pre-requisites for promoting **self-development.**

55th STANDARD

To ensure the Group's **Survival, Growth** and **Perpetuity,** each Individual must assimilate the following fact: **the moment the Individual sets a limit, he will only progress when he goes beyond that limit.**

7.   THE GROUP'S IMAGE

56th STANDARD

Just as the **results** of the Odebrecht Group Companies are a **consequence** of the **effective coordination** and **synergetic integration** of the Human Beings who comprise them, so their image results from what these Human Beings project **individually** and **collectively** in the eyes of their Clients, Partners and other Suppliers, and the Community as a whole.

57th STANDARD

While winning over and satisfying their Clients, the Group's Members must also fulfill the Community's **ethical** and **moral** standards by being **model Citizens** who are responsible for applying and adding value to the **Odebrecht Hallmark.**

This truth must guide the **attitudes** and **behaviors** of each of the Group's Members in public and in private.

8. HEALTH, SAFETY, QUALITY OF LIFE AND THE ENVIRONMENT

58th STANDARD

The **Odebrecht Entrepreneurial Technology** is opposed to any form of "waste," and therefore values **individual responsibility** in each and every sphere of operation.

From this perspective, the Odebrecht Group's Shareholders believe that it is "wasteful" to neglect the **health** and **safety** of its Members as well as the **quality of life** and **Environmental preservation** of the **Communities** in which they work.

59th STANDARD

The Odebrecht Group rejects "paternalism," because it impedes the full exercise of civil rights and duties and the blossoming of individual initiative.

Within the Group Companies, Health and Safety are viewed as conditions that are basic and inherent to quality of life. The promotion of these conditions in a safe working environment is essential to the Individual's professional, emotional and financial fulfillment.

The organization's growth ensues from the development of the People who comprise it. Therefore, Health Promotion and the Prevention of Health and Safety Risks must be continually practiced to improve and fully develop their individual potential.

STANDARDS FOR APPLYING THE ODEBRECHT ENTREPRENEURIAL TECHNOLOGY
Operating Standards
151

60th STANDARD

The Group's Leaders are responsible for creating the conditions for harmoniously integrating the interests of their Clients, Communities and the Individuals who comprise them with the interests of the Shareholders, based on the aim of constantly promoting health and quality of life, preventing risks and damage, and preserving the Environment.

Each Leader must have a proactive, educational and motivating attitude in order to lead each of his Partners to the awareness that they are the agents of their own future and therefore responsible for

- assimilating the culture of promotion and prevention in the areas of Health, Safety and the Environment;

- using resources, including health care services, offered by the State and/or the Company (when necessary); and

- constantly developing their own health in order to prevent risks and damage resulting from their lifestyle.

The adequate fulfillment of these conditions will depend upon the **maturity** of these People and the **quality** of the relationship between them, their Leaders, Clients and other members of their Communities.

Composição, Fotolitos e Impressão

Avenida Iemanjá, 365 - Jardim Armação
41715-320 - Salvador - Bahia
Tel. (71) 3371-1665 - Fax (71) 3371-6041
pagrafica@uol.com.br